Bhima Bhoi
A Multifaceted Genius

Editor
Prof. Harischandra Sahoo

VIDYA
PUBLISHING INC.

Vidya Publishing Inc.
Toronto, Canada || Bhubaneswar, Odisha

BHIMA BHOI

A Multifaceted Genius

Edited by :

Prof. Harischandra Sahoo
41, Arnapurna Residential Complex
Shelter Chhak, Tulsipur, Cuttack - 753008
Mob.: 9438408465
E-mail : harissahoo9@gmail.com

ISBN : 978-1-998475-99-5

First Edition : September, 2025

Published by : Dr. Tanmay Panda & Dr. Sunanda Mishra Panda
Vidya Publishing Inc.,
Toronto, Canada || Bhubaneswar, Odisha
Website : www.vidyapublishing.com
Email : vidyapublishinginc@gmail.com
Cell : +1 6478389884

Odisha Contact : Nirmalya Garden, Plot 516/1719, House 10,
KIIT Post Office, Patia, Bhubaneswar - 751024
Cell : +91 8984131810

Cover Design : Sasikanta Rout, Cuttack
Printed at : Biswanath Enterprises, India

Price : ₹ 250/-

Dedicated to
Droupadi Murmu
Her Excellency,
The President of India
for her keen interest in
Bhima Bhoi.

Editor's Note

In this volume, attempt has been made to unravel the multifaceted personality of saint-poet Bhima Bhoi. He is an extra ordinary poet. His writings are spontaneous expression of his heart for a social revolution. He encountered the blind-beliefs, superstitions and exploitation of the so-called higher ruling class and the brahmins which disrupted the social harmony and development. This book is an attempt to explore Bhima Bhoi's view on different aspects of social evils. Bhima's aim was not to propound a philosophical doctrine about Mahimā Dharma, rather to reach the common man through colloquial language, poiṇting out that everyone is potentially divine. He wanted to inculcate this spiritual consciousness that everyone irrespective of caste, creed and sex can reach the perfection of his personality. His purpose was not confined to relieve the suffering of human beings but all living beings where the '*Śūnya Purusha*' is present.

The articles contained in this book highlights different aspects like metaphysics, ethics and the means (the *Sādhanā*) for the human beings who are considered to be the highest in the evolutionary process. So human beings should shoulder the responsibility of relieving the sufferings of all beings. The book hightlights the philosophy of Bhima Bhoi from a different perspective which is rarely found in *Santhas*. Bhima was a *Santha* (saint) in true sense of the term as he did not want salvation for himself but the upliftment and emancipation of all beings from the sorrows and sufferings they face. The term 'salvation' has different connotation here. It is not other-wordly but refers to the present world where we live in.

Bhima's writings aimed at rigorous practical life based on genuine metaphysics where he has explained that the reality is pervaded in everything; animate or inanimate, biotic or abiotic community. His view aimed at the mitigation of sorrows and sufferings from the universe.

Pabitra Mohan Nayak in his article "The Relevance of Bhima Bhoi to present social context" calls Mahimā Dharma as "Satya Mahimā Dharma". Bhima Bhoi, ardent disciple of Mahimā Swāmi prays the Guru for a harmonious and balanced society, where there would be no barrier among the rich and the poor, touchables and untouchables, bourgeoise and proletariat. There should be a classless society where all castes are one as all are the children of God. Bhima speaks of one humanity, without any division. Women should be given freedom. Bhima is a champion of women emancipation since no woman is inferior to man. Bhima had a vision of one earth, one family and one future.

Ishita Banerjee Dube in her article Bhima "Bhoi : Ethnographic Histories" gives a historial approach to the subject. As a young research scholar 30 years ago she had visited Khaliapāli Āshram in Sonepur district. She was surprised to see the changes undergone in the Āshram. The Āshram of Bhima Bhoi has been changed into a Samādhipitha. In the mean time, a lot of literature have been written on Bhima Bhoi and Bhima's Granthāvali have been published. Bhima has been instituationalised and he has become a seminal figure, a radical national poet and pride of Odisha in histories of literature in Odia language. His poems have been published over centuries.

Dhaneswar Sahoo in his article "Bhima Bhoi : Humanism and World Peace" emphasises on the creative poetic talent of Bhima Bhoi who was agasint the evil practices like untocuchability and social division due to caste hierarchy. His poetic vision is not confined to devotion and glory of Lord Mahimā Swāmi rather he was a humanist and having humanitarian vision of life as he expressed his concern for world peace.

Harischandra Sahoo is his article, entitled "Bhima Bhoi : The Propagator of *Jñāna Misrā Bhakti*" advocates that bhakti is a mode of self-realization along with Karma and Jñāna. Bhima advocates Bhakti Mārga that elevates man to a status of higher spiritual level. Although Bhima advocates bhakti as a means to reach the godhead, he has not denounced karma and Jñāna altogether. A hardcore Sādhanā is needed so that right knowledge (Sadjñāna) is possible. Right knowledge is not possible without bhakti. A true Guru is capable of initiating the vision of reality in the mind of disciple so that Jñāna Misrā Bhakti will lead him to become a Samadarshi and the world becomes a family for him to lead a happy life.

Subhasis Sahoo and Sital Mohanty in the article "Framing Faith : Towards a Sociology of Mahimā Cult" express their finding in the field research from 2019 to 2020 and discussed the universalism of Mahimā Dharma, Philosophical worldview of Mahimā Dharma, the behavioural aspect of Bhima Bhoi and institutional factor behind Bhima Bhoi as a personality. To be precise their approach to Bhima Bhoi and Mahima Dharma is analysed from sociological stand-point. They have explained the mysticism and asceticism involved (in Mahimā Dharma). Bhima Bhoi was not an ascetic (Sanyāsi) rather he was a *gruhi-bhakta*. They conclude the paper with the remark that Mahimā Dharma is a synthesis of monism of Advaita Vedānta and Śūnya Vāda of Buddhism. It depicts a humanstic approach to life with emphasis on equality, justice and social obligations.

Chittaranjan Misra's article "Bhima Bhoi's Spiritual Vision and Social Aspiration in *Ādianta Gitā*" which is a piece of wisdom having 12 chapters in the form of dialogue between the Jiva (individual self) and Parama (the supreme reality). Jiva is inquisitive to know about the nature of self. The literal meaning of '*Ā*di" is beginning and 'Anta" mean the end. It depicts the theory of creation (cosmology). While discussing about theory of creation, Bhima explains the relation between the husband *(Juba)* and the wife *(Jubati)*. Such a description of love – making is found in Vātsāyana's *Kāma-Sūtra.*

Chittaranjan Bhoi presents the translation of "Bangala Ātha Bhajan" under the title "Bengali Sacred Hymns". Since there are many Bengali devotees for them, Bhima has composed these bhajans (eight in number). The central theme of the title is same as *'Stuti Chintāmaṇi'*. Like Sri Aurobindo, Bhima Bhoi considers the creation as the Leelā of the śūnya Purusha. From Indian mythology, Bhima takes the concept of Trinity i.e. Brahmā, Vishnu and Shiva. Mahimā Swāmi is above the trinity whose abode is Mahā śūnya. It is bhakti mārga that helps one to realize the ultimate reality and only a true guru is the path –finder.

Sarat Chandra Panigrahi in his article "Guru Tattva and Nāma Tattva in the philosophy of Bhima Bhoi" emphasizes on the key role played by the spiritual mentor (guru) for realization of the God-head. Guru is the path-finder but the disciple has to undertake the spiritual journey by himself. He has to make self –effort. Jñāna and bhakti are blended together to have the self-realisation. Chanting the nāma of Alekha is a means to reach the ultimate goal.

Anjali Mohapatra's article entitled "Philosophy of Bhima Bhoi and Jagannāth Dāsa" depicts the similar views of Jagannāth Dāsa and Bhima Bhoi regarding *Piṇḍa – Brahmaṇḍa Tattva*, theory of creation, Bhakti as the easiest path for spiritual perfection, the *vital* role of Guru in the field of Sādhanā. Both of them point out the unique synthesis of knowledge, action and devotion. Both are humanists in the real sense of the term.

Laxmimani Majhi in her article "Karma, Jñāna and Bhakti in Philospphy of Bhima Bhoi and Kabir : A Comparative Study" offers a comparative study of Bhima Bhoi and Saint-poet Kabir. Both Bhima and Kabir belong to *santha* tradition. Her study clearly explains the similarities between the two great poets. Both of them expressed their concern for the upliftment of the downtrodden class and emphasized on social change. Both of them propagated *Bhakti Mārga* as means of attainment of the godhead.

Satyananda Swain's article "Bhima Bhoi's *Stuti Chintāmaṇi* (Gems of soulful prayer): Testament of a Poet" offers an analysis of Bhima's *Magnum Opus "Stuti Chintāmaṇi"* a Bible for Mahima followers. He has discussed in details the different aspects of Mahimā Dharma in his article. He explains the role of a *gruhi* (household) to perform while initiated to Mahimā fold. What is the role of monks, wondering mendicants and what is Guru Dharma etc. all these issues are discussed elaborately by him.

This book is an humble tribute to the life and literary legacy of Bhima Bhoi, the saint-poet from the remote yet spiritually rich region of Western Odisha. It is an attempt to acquaint readers with his profound vision and enduring contributions to society.

I extend my deepest gratitude to Prof. Deepak Kumar Behera, Prof. N. Nagaraju, Prof. Debasish Bandopadhyay, Prof. S.C. Panigrahi, Dr. Chittaranjan Misra, and Dr. Chittaranjan Bhoi whose intellectual support and encouragement have been imperative in shaping this work. Each esteemed contributor is a fellow traveller in this journey of exploring Bhima Bhoi's wisdom and compassionate voice.

Special thanks to my student, Mr. Suresh Kumar Pradhan for his timely assistance throughout the preparation of the manuscript. I am also grateful to Mr. Bibhu Prasad Sahoo for typing the manuscript and Mr. Sashikanta Rout for his thoughtful design of the cover page.

My heartfelt appreciation goes to my wife Bidyutprava, and daughter Dr. Sonali Priyadarshini whose constant encouragement has kept me anchored and motivated.

I also thank Dr. Tanmaya Panda and Mrs. Sunanda Mishra Panda of Vidya Publications for their enthusiastic support in bringing this work for publication.

This book is the outcome of shared efforts and a collective pursuit of understanding. I welcome constructive suggestions and positive feedback from readers to further enrich the future editions.

Guru Bhrama Mahimā Alekh!

Cuttack
27.08.2025

Harischandra Sahoo
Editor

•

CONTENTS...

Relevance of Mahimā Dharma to the present social context

Pabitra Mohan Nayak

Mahimā Dharma is *Satya Dharma.* Look at the titles of some books in Mahimā religion published in 20th Century. Bābā Baisnava Charana's *Satya Mahimā Dharma Pratibodha* (1977) Bābā Mahindra's *Satya Mahimā Dharma* in Bengali (1956), *Satya Dharmara Samkhipta Itihāsa, Viswakalyāṇa Pathe Satya Mahimā Dharma (1957), Satyamahimā Dharmara Nitiniyama (1958) and Satya Mahima Dharma Parichaya* (1960), Bābā Biswanath's *Bhāgabatasāra Satyadharma* (1955), *An Exposition of Satya Mahimā Dhrama* (1956), *Satya Mahimā Dharmaka Swarup, Satya Mahimā Dharma Pradipa, Satya Mahimā Dharma Pratipādaka* (1971), *Satya Mahimā Dharmara Itihāsa* (1978) and *Satya Mahimā Dhrama Parichaya (1982). Parichaya, Pradipa, Praatibodhaka* and *Pratipadaka* are variables. The common factor is Satya Mahimā Dharma. What is Satya? What is Truth said Jesting Pilate but did not stay for an answer (Bacon). Truth to Christ was untruth to Pilate. He sent him to the cross. Long before Einstein, power proved the relativity of truth. Truth may be the antonym of falsehood (*Satyam Bṛuyat*). It may something permanent, unchanging in a world of changes and chances, an eternal varity in a world of Heraclitean flux. It may be *dharma, Nyāya. Satya Meba Jayate*. The moon to Galileo was a dead heavenly body revealed through his telescope, which shocked the religionists of Rome. A blasphemy, something irreligious which carried the penalty of death. By the time, he was cross questioned, he had grown wiser and more pragmatic. What do you see on the moon, Galileo? I, I see angels with wings. You would have said aliens, Galileo was saved, Chirst died for Truth, Galileo survived through untruth. To Bhima (Bhoi) truth is life, untruth, death. Truth is God, as it was to Gandhi, God is Truth as it was to the *Upanishads*, Lord forgive us, we mean what we do not say, we say what we do not mean: *Michha Kahibāku Kiān Daribi, Sata Kahi Kahi Muhi Maribi.*

Why should I be afraid of falsehood? Why should I die for speaking the truth? To live for truth and die for truth, it is implied in *Stuti Chintāmaṇi:*

> "*Satyare Maribi, Satyare Taribi*
> *Ehi ajñā heu mote.*

To a Mahimite, truth is neither a scientist's nor a philosopher's truth. It is the ultimate reality, *Param Brahman* as Bhima Bhoi would have it. "Oh, I plunge into the sea of Brahman! I am confident observes Bhima Bhoi in *Stuti Chintāmaṇi*, When I die, I will merge with *Brahman*. "Half truth and hersy, hypocrisy, hearesay, robbery and burglary, Thou shalt not steal" (The Bible).

Mahimāism believed in one God, one law, one Universe. God is one, one not many. (*Ekoham*) and He is formless and nameless, No appearance, no attributes, *Nirbikāra Nirābayaba, Niskāma, Nirguṇa Brahman*. He is *Śūnya Brahma, śūnya, śūnya, Mahāśūnya*. He is *prakriti*. He is *Purusha*. He is the sky and the sea, master and slave, Guru and Sisya, Sun and Moon *(Brahma Nirupaṇa Gitā)*. The *Vedas* stopped with the Trinity. Bhima went beyond *mahā-nitya mandala*, the land of the Eternal present where there is neither light nor sound, hunger nor thirst, Sun or Moon; "*Na tatra Surjyo Bhāti, na Chandra*

Tārakam". This *Abhaya mandira* is built without walls, plastered without lime, roofed without beams (*Bhajanamālā*).

God is up there. God is down here in the heart. Brahma in the *navi*, *Jagannath* in the heart and *Shiva* in the *throat*. Then why do you go to temples? The poet wonders. Look at the living humans worshipping dead idols, praying save us, save us! If the sky is the head and earth his foot stool, why do you seek him within temple walls, in craven images of wood and stone? If he is not there, why do you visit Badrināth or Ramnāth or Somnāth? If he has neither hands, nor feet, eyes nor ears, why this offering, this *pujā pārvaṇa?* Look within and offer your devotion. You need not seek Him. He will come as he came that fateful *Kārtik Dasami* Night to Kankanapadā to bless Bhima Bhoi. This is salvation made easy and universal, for the physically challenged, economically handicapped, socially disadvantaged.

Mahimāism is a non-idolatrous religion, and Bhima was an uncompromising iconoclast. He wanted to break down all idols so that people would worship *śūnya Brahman*. If we believe with H.K. Mahatab, that Bhima had visited Puri to have a *darsan* of Lord Jagannāth, that he was a devotee of Jagannāth Dāsa and Jagannāth Dāsa was a devotee of Lord Jagannāth, we will commit a logical fallacy, the fallacy of *undistributed middle*. Read *Nirveda Sādhana* and *Sruti Nishedha Gitā* and a couple of poems included in *Bhajanamālā*

"Se yadi Jagannath hontā
Akai thābe ki rahantā !"

To demolish the idol of Jagannath is to demolish all idols and proclaim the glory of *śūnya Brahma*. Therefore, while the editor of *Sulabha Samāchār* of Bengal admired the audacity of the tribals to break and burn the images of Shri Mandir. Gouri Shankar Ray, called them a drunken, uncivilized lot and asked Govt. to clap them in prison.

Like the Arya Samāj, Brahmo Samāj, Prāthanā Samāj, Sikhs and Muslims, Mahimā Dharma does not believe in idol worship. Only in Hindu religion, we have panthenon of gods and goddesses. This leads to conflicts and controversies among *the Vaisnavas, the Shaivas, the Gānapatyas* and the Shāktas. Mahimā Dharma therefore, believed in one God, *Śūnya Brahma.*

And if God is one, why should castes be many? When *pralaya* comes, blasts Bhima, I will see which fatherless boy keeps his caste then? There is only one caste; the caste of humanity. Bhima had seen the tyranny of kings at *Rairakhol* and Sonepur. He had seen the exploitation of *Pandās, Padhihāris, Pujāris* and *Purohits.* Therefore, he was up against kings and brāhmins. They were the upper castes of the society and they dictated terms to the lowly and the low. They have erected walls between the haves and the have-nots, the bourgeoise and the proletariats, the touchables and the untouchables. They forebade them to draw and drink water from the same well. They banished them from the day. As if, to see them is to spoil the day. Besides, casteism hampers the unity, solidarity and fellow-feeling in the society. So he declared, leave casteism for salvation or salvation for casteism:

Jāti Khojile Mukti Nāhi
Mukti Khojile Jāti Kāhin?

Had we listened to him, India would have advanced towards a classless, casteless society by now. Rightly Gandhi called untouchability, a stain on India's forehead. If all men are children of God, why should there be distance and difference between the caste and a differcnt caste? One remembers John Donne, *"No man is an island. Each man is a part of the continent, a piece of the main. Each death diminishes me because I am involved in mankind. Therefore, never ask to know for whom the bell tolls, it tolls for thee."* Mahimā Dharma too had this worldview or *Weltanschauung*.

All castes are one. All men are *amritasya putraḥ*; Children of immortality Despite the abolition of untouchability in 1950, 55 years after Bhima's death SC/ST Reservation prevention of Atrocity Act 1989 and incentive for intercaste marriage by some states, the situation has not visibly improved. Yet Bhima Bhoi's pain has not gone in vain.

The next question is the woman question. They say feminism is essentially an occidental concept. But it is incorrect. Long before Aphra Behn flew her first feminist flag in 17th century Europe against the unmitigated autocratic authoritarianism of a phallocentric world, long before the suffragist Sophia asserted, woman not inferior to man (1739) or Merechal asked, shall woman learn the alphabet (1801) long before Naomi, Lucretia, the Amazons, Penelope, St. Joan, Petrarch's Laura beautiful ignoramuses were born long before Tagore adored woman as "*Ardheka Mānasi Tumi Ardheka Kalpanā*", long before the daughters of the redoubtable Charlemangne learnt to spell their names, we had our *Gārgi, Maitreyi* and *Lopāmudrā* of the Vedic times holding sessions on the Vedas and the Vedāntas, we had *Sitā* defying the demon king of Lanka to defend her chastity, we had *yojanagandhā* dictating terms of her marriage to Rajā *Sāntanu*, we had *Draupadi* bathing her hair in the blood of *Duhsāsana* who had tried to disrobe her in the *Rājasabhā*. While women of the West were branded cats, Hell cats, Malignant cats (Clare Booth; The Women, Foreword,

1937), we addressed them as *ardhānginis*, and gods worshipped Siva as *Ardhanāriswara*. Rightly does Manu aver,

Yatra Naryāstu Pujyante
Ramante Tatra Debatāh

While there in the West, Alice Miller in the *Women Voter* presents the gullibility and stupidity of woman in a dialogue between the clever male and foolish female who believes in marriage and motherhood as late as 1915.

I am cleverer than you
: Very true, very true
I am braver, too, by far
: So you are, so you are
I can use my mind a lot
: We cannot, we cannot
Men adore your lack of mind
: Oh, how kind, how kind
You do very well without
: Not a doubt, not a doubt
You have hardly any sense
: What eloquence, what eloquence
Yet your moral sense is weaker
: Is'nt he a charming speaker!

Nearer home, Bhima unlike his Guru at Jorandā flung the gate of Khalliāpāli *Āshram* open to women. He accepted *Annapurnā*, a Brāhmin widow as his consort, made her *Ādimātā* of the *āshram* and had four more-*Rohini*, *Sumedhā*, *Saraswati* and *Subarnā*. We had another Bhima later in India. Bhim Rao Ambedkar who married a Brāhmin woman to wreak revenge on brāhminical orthodoxy and changed to Buddhism out of his disgust with the caste-ridden Hinduism. To Bhima, a man's worldly as well as yogic life is incomplete without a woman. This completion complex is reflected in *Ādi-Anta-Gitā* and *Rasarkeli, Dālkhai, Jāiphula* and *Chautisās* marked by unconcealed expressions of unabashed sex in the passionate, sensuous poetry of his warm youth. So much so that some Western critics trace the influence of *Sahajāyana Buddhism-* from sex to salvation- in these works, which is dubitable and debatable. In one of the most powerful metaphysical *chautisās* Bhima blatantly faces Mahimā, Lord! why did you create men and women, if you don't want them to come together? Bhima gave women their full measure of freedom, their power and their prestige in the land of Laxminkara and the *Sat Bahens*, seven tantric sisters more powerful than men. On the day of *Māgha Purnimā*, Annapurnā and Bhima used to sit on the altar, 108 lamps burning on the steps and offerings made by men and women.

Women are born free but are still in chains. Specially in the African continent and Muslim dominated Middle East. In India economic inequality, domestic atrocity and gender discrimination still dog their steps, yet behind Annie Besant's efforts for women voting rights in 1885, a decade before Bhima's death, formation of National Council of Women in 1921, All India Women's Conference in 1927 and 1930, the Hindu marriage Act, the Hindu Succession Act of 1956, Dowry prohibition Act 1981 and abolition of "Tripple Talāk" and reservation of women's seats in the parliament in 2023, we see the shadow of Mahima Dharma.

Thus Bhima Bhoi will continue to live in the memories of men not for the lyrical simplicity and intensity of his poetry or his versatility in versification, not for his anti-casteist stance or non-idolatrous ideas, not for his pioneering role in women's lib, not for his *niṣkāma karmayoga* in the midst of a falling world, but for the verities and values he has left behind for us, humans we who have come a long way from the Garden of Eden to the Brave New World. But we still incorrigibly remain a bundle of anger and greed, envy and enmity, hate and hunger, sans the values of fellow-feeling, human sympathy, compassion, truth and non-violence. Mahimāism, thus, is a mother of this cosmic consciousness, world vision of one earth, one family, one future; in a word of the values of humanitarianism.

Today when a low-born family is boycotted in a village, its light and water connections cut off, or a frail sickly wife is beaten and driven out or even an encaged parrot frets for freedom, a white little rabbit lifts a cry somewhere, when innocent lives are lost in senseless violence of ruthless war, when the high flood swells and sweeps the earth, we will surely see two skinny arms raised in the posture of prayer to the Creator of the universe or when the rising flame of war amidst the blasts of bombs tearing a whole civilization in the midst of smoking ruins and ceaseless missiles, we remember you, Bhima Bhoi, the silent saint of Khalliāpāli. Allow me to recall through the last line of a poem, "Still falls the rain". Edith Sitwell had composed in the thick of World War-II in 1942, still do I love, still shed my innocent light, my blood for thee! Which mingles with Bhima's hymn this side of the British Channel, *let my life be hurled into hell, but let the universe be redeemed.* Who can say this except the one whose heart holds the universe?

REFERENCES :

(1) A. Eschmann, et al, *The Cult of Jagannath*, New Delhi, Manohar, 1978.

(2) Asiatic Society of Bengal, *Proceedings*, Jan'1982.

(3) Banerjee, Ishita, *Jagannath Revised*, New Delhi : Manohar, 2007.

—— *Popular Religions and Ascetic Practises*, New Delhi Manohar, 2008.

(4) N.N. Basu, *Modern Buddhism & Its followers in Odisha*, Calcutta, 1911.

(5) Beltz, Johannes, Asectic, *Layman or Rebellious Guru* in *Popular Religions and Ascetic Practices* – by Ishita B. Dubey.

(6) Baumer, Bettina, *Tāntric Elements in Bhima Bhoi's Ocuvre (Ibid.)*

(7) Bell, Catherine, *Ritual Theory, Ritual Practices*, New Delhi : OUP, 1992.

(8) Buckland, C.E., *Bengal under Lt. Governors in Global Perspectives*, London : 2006.

(9) Cunningham, Lawrence, *The Meaning of Saints*, Harper & Row, 1980.

(10) Chatterjee Partha & Gyanendra Pandey, *Subaltern Studies* Vol.-8, II, New Delhi OUP.

(11) Das, C.R., *Odishara Mahimā Dharma*, Calcutta, Viswa Bharati, 1952.

—— *Studies in Medieval Religion & Literature of Orissa*, Viswabharati Annals, Vol-IV.

(12) Das Rasbihari. *Sri Guru Mahātmya*, 1973.

(13) Hess, Linda, *Kabir's Rough Rhetoric,* Motilal Benarassi Das, 1907.

(14) Jacobson, Janet & Ann Pellegrini (ed.) *Secularism Durham* : Duke Univ. Press, 2008.

(15) *Jagannath Temple Correspondences*, Acc No. 432, Odisha State Archives.

(16) Mansingh, Mayadhar, *The History of Oriya Literature*, New Delhi : Sahitya Academy, 1962.

—— *The Saga of Land of Jagannath*, 1971.

(17) Mazumdar, B.C., *"Alekhism in Sonepur in Sambalpur Tract"*. Calcutta: Brahmo Mission Press, 1911.

(18) Mill, J.S., *The History of British India*, Vol-I, London: 1840.

(19) Nandy, Ashis, *The Intimate Enemy*, New Delhi, OUP, 1994.

(20) Nayak, P.M., "Mo Jivan Pachhe Narke Padithāu", *Santha Kabirnka Jibana Nātaka*, Cuttack, Arya.

———, *The Voice of Silence*, Odisha Sahitya Academy, BBSR, 2001.

——, *Subltern Voice*, Odisha Sahitya Academy, BBSR, 2016.

——, (ed.), *Bhima Bhoi Granthāvali,* Cuttack, Friends, (2018 – 20)

(21) Sing, K.S., *Tribal Society in India*, New Delhi, Manohar, 1985.

(22) Shyamaghana – *Alekha Leelā*, Cuttack, Dharma Grantha Store, 1982.

(23) O'Malley - *Utkal Dipikā*, June 1, 1867.

(24) O'Malley, *Sambalpur Dist. Gazetter*, 1909.

(25) Omvedt, Gail, *Dalits & Dalits Democratic Revolution*, London, 1994.

•

Bhima Bhoi: Ethnographic Histories*

Ishita Banerjee-Dube

In March 2022, I re-visited the Khalliāpāli *Āshram* of Bhima Bhoi after three decades. Even though I had heard about the changes resulting from an appreciative acknowledgement and a certain canonisation of Bhima Bhoi in western Odisha, I was surprised by the transformation of a difficult to reach and somewhat forlorn āshram into a vibrant, well-maintained complex, with well-laid out pathways leading to the shrines, painted red, the office, and to the accommodation for *bhaktas* (followers/devotees). The unkempt grassy patches that surrounded the shrines have turned into green lawns. The walls of the buildings are adorned with different couplets of Bhima Bhoi. Most striking for me were the drawings of Bhima Bhoi with the emblematic palm-leaf like a halo around his head. When I had visited the *Āshram* in the early 1990s, the silver sandals (*khatau*) used by Bhima Bhoi kept in a shrine were the only visible symbol of the mortal presence of Bhima Bhoi, the poet-philosopher and teacher, venerated by his followers.

When and why did the drawings come up? Why were they needed? And what did they stand for? In response to my queries, a member of the Bhima Bhoi *Samādhipitha* Trust and

---

**I express my thanks to Prof. Deepak Kumar Behera, Prof. N. Nagraju, Prof. Harischandra Sahoo and Prof. P.K. Panda for their keen interest in Bhima Bhoi and Mahimā Dharma.*

Renu Nani, Renuka Misra, a scholar and a senior teacher of Sonepur College who had accompanied me to the *Āshram* thirty years back and went with me in 2022, informed me that the drawings were expressions of the devotees' emotive imaginings of their *guru*; they are not real-life portraits of Bhima Bhoi.

Indeed, the change from *Āshram* to *Samādhipitha* is significant. While it is true that the *Āshram* compound had Bhima Bhoi, his spiritual consort Mā Annapurnā, and his son Kapileswar interred next to the shrines from the beginning, the āshram had, as yet, not acquired sufficient significance as a sacred place and a site of pilgrimage, similar to the Mahimāgādi in Joranda, Dhenkanal. The *Samādhi* (memorial) of Mahimā Swāmi, it bears mention, was constructed at a time of crisis after the unexpected death of Mahimā Swāmi—perceived by the disciples as an incarnation of the Absolute— to provide a disparate group of followers of a mobile, detached preceptor a permanent and sedentary symbol to cement and hold together the community of believers. The refurbished and reconfigured *Samādhipitha* in Khalliāpāli represents a similar institutionalisation of Bhima Bhoi in the public arena, and makes one ponder why it was necessary and what its implications are for the adherents of the faith.

Members of the *Samādhipitha* Trust and the current head of the āshram, in addition to welcoming us with the Sambalpuri *chādar* and offering us a sumptuous mid-day meal, also presented me with a copy of the journal *Mahimā*, launched during the *Māgipurnimā* (full-moon in the month of *māgh*, January-February) celebration in 2019. Congratulatory messages and photos of the Governor's visit to the *Samādhipitha* and other important events there constitute half of the journal. The other half is composed of brief essays on Bhima Bhoi that range from the *'The Humanism of Bhima Bhoi'* written by the late Sadanand Agrawal whom I had met in the early 1990s, to *Rāmāyana kathā* in Bhima Bhoi's compositions and the presence of Marxist ideas in them. Once again, I was reminded of the divergent perceptions and analyses of Bhima Bhoi and his compositions that have been a constant feature of literary and scholarly works related to Bhima Bhoi since the beginning of the twentieth century.

I was emotionally saturated and overwhelmed. The revisit, the meeting with Renu Nani, the presence of Dr. Fanindam Deo with his family that brought back memories of our joyous days at the Indian Institute of Advanced Study in Shimla, and most of all, the radical transformation in the Khalliāpāli *Āshram* into a *Samādhipitha* together with a shift in imaginings of Bhima Bhoi, caused a vague sense of unease.

Back in my room in Sambalpur that evening, I tried to reflect on my various impressions and uncertain reaction to them. Why was I unsure about the effect of this institutionalisation and visualisation of Bhima Bhoi and his *Samādhipitha*? Was I not trying to hang on to the nostalgia of my old days of intensive field-work when there was no paved road to the Khalliāpāli *Āshram*? After all, in my doctoral dissertation and even more in my book published several years later I had argued that Bhima Bhoi, a creative genius, could not be contained by the dictates of any single faith and that his compositions were amenable to a wide range of understandings and apprehensions. Why then, was I troubled by recently evolving perceptions and practices?

This self-reflection and criticism enabled me to decide on the theme of today's discussion. It goes back to the basic questions of how we address the subjects of our research and what we learn from them and how? Does ethnography in the anthropological sense of 'immersion' in the life-worlds *(lebenswelt)* of our subjects that allow entry into the layered and mixed-up realities of social life, in conjunction with a constant self-warning about not converting our subjects into objects of research,enable a more nuanced and respectful ethnographic history?Drawing upon my own study and musings over the past three decades, I attempt to offer a panorama of the varied perceptions, assessments and appropriations of Bhima Bhoi, his life and works by *bhaktas* and scholars to offer a diffused and a tentative response to the question.

Bhima Bhoi in written records :

The first problem that confronts us when we try to get access to the world of a legendary poet-saint such as Bhima Bhoi is that of the sources. The predominantly oral world of a late nineteenth century poet and his followers become available to us only when they are inscribed in writing by colonial administrators and Baptist missionaries working in Odisha, as well as in the only vernacular newspaper of the time, the *Utkal Deepikā.*

Government reports on the 'Followers of Alekh' drawn upafter the 'attack' on the temple Jagannāth in Puri on 1 March 1881,point toSambalpur as the region where the Kumbhipatiā Dharma had most of its followers. This is borne out by the fact that only the Census of the Central Provinces of 1881 provided separate statistics on the Kumbhipatiās of Sambalpur in its tables. And reports of colonial officials and *tehsildārs*(revenue officers) of the tributary states, without connecting Bhima Bhoi to the 'attack', mentioned him as the composer of a book of 'songs and dialogues interpreting the truth of *Alekh* that was widely used by the followers of the faith.

'Kumbhipatiā Bābāji', a feature in the *Utkal Deepikā* of 19 November 1881, informed the readers that Bhima Khond was the leader of Kumbhipatiās, 'a community that exists in Sambalpur district'. It also affirmed that even though the Dharma was first preached by Alekh Swāmi in Banki, it soon 'gained special spread in the district of Sambalpur' where people of all castes except the Brāhmans adopted the faith. The daily commended Bhima for being 'very intelligent'. Born blind and with 'no formal education' he has composed some songs and hymns in praise of God whose beautiful style can hardly be matched by the most educated.' The very next sentence, however, condemned him for getting a woman pregnant through *pāpa praṇaya* ('illicit love'), a fact that had annoyed many adherents and caused dissension with the faith. The report did not fail to point out, however, that the followers who remained with Bhima Bhoi, venerated him 'like god'. This was reflected in the daily morning ritual when Bhima Bhoi and his wife sat on a *bedi* (raised platform) and the *bhaktas* circumambulated it, washed Bhima's feet with milk and then drank it. This found a more elaborate retelling in the Foreword written by Karunakar Sahu, the compiler of *Bhaktakabi Bhima Bhoinka Granthābali,* in the new edition published by the Dharma Grantha Store in 1978.

Baptist missionaries working in Sambalpur referred approvingly in their annual report of 1881-1882 to the fact that the 'Kumbhipatiās' were growing in number. For the messengers of Christ, this was a welcome sign of continued reactionary [*sic*] movement against the grosser forms of idolatry'. By 1887-88, however, Bhima Bhoi had become an 'impostor', a master of 'blasphemous pretensions', who gave himself out to be 'a new incarnation', an *anādi avatāra* (incarnation without beginning), who had appeared on earth 'to inaugurate a new dispensation'.

A considered examination of these ambivalent contemporary reports enables us to get glimpses of the oral circulation of Bhima Bhoi's compositions among his *bhaktas* and their myriad collective understandings of Bhima Bhoi's message and life that made them deify their master despite his non-conformist lifestyle. Why were administrators, missionaries and the Odia literati perturbed by the fact that he had more than one consort? Is it because of their own moral prioritisation of celibacy among 'religious' leaders? And what was it in Bhima Bhoi's life and preaching that made him immensely appealing to large groups of subordinate women and men in western Odisha? Bhima Bhoi, as indicated above, was an enigmatic figure whose life and message were pliable enough to be understood and set to work in divergent ways.

It is likely that his ingenious compositions that combined different trends of thought current in Odisha to speak of an Absolute who was at once all-powerful and indescribable and accessible to all through devotion, and insisted on the urgency of taking shelter at the feet of the Absolute to avoid destruction in *Kaliyug*, offered solace and hope to marginal and oppressed groups of peoples who laboured under the hierarchies of caste, class, privilege and ritual status? In order toget a sense of how they understood Bhima Bhoi's lyrics that spoke against caste and a belief in idols, and his practice of living with women,we need to read the sparse yet varied written records with a critical and imaginative ethnographic eye and sensibility.

It bears mention that the ambiguity in regard to an unlettered poet of low birth reflected in late-nineteenth-century reports got transformed into admiration at the turn of the century. An essay titled 'Bhima Bhoi's acquisition of knowledge' written by a senior official of the court of Sonepur and published in the literary magazine *Mukur* in 1908, expressed the author's desire to make Bhima Bhoi and 'his religion' known to readers.The essay was followed by two influential texts of N.N. Vasu, a senior administrator-cum scholar of the state of Mayurbhanj. Vasu's*The Archeological Survey of Mayurbhanja*, and *The Modern Buddhism and its Followers in Orissa* published in 1911,established Bhima Bhoi as the leader of the 'sect' and praised him for his 'immortal instruction' that helped spread 'real knowledge' and had the 'mighty pillars of the caste system' stoop at his feet, 'even though the blood of the low kandha ran in his veins.'

B. C. Mazumdar, another official of the Sonepur court, in addition to commending Bhima Bhoi for his charming and commanding personality, also credited him with the leadership of the attack on the Jagannāth temple, a fact that according to Mazumdar was corroborated by Government records, do not corroborate the 'fact', but it is instructive that texts published within a decade and a half of Bhima Bhoi's death linked him to the incident of 1 March 1881.

Bhima Bhoi in the quotidian arena :

It is in order here to ask why B.C. Mazumdar and subsequent government records credited Bhima Bhoi with inspiring his followers to go to Puri and destroy the lifeless images of the Jagannāth trinity. Did such an idea stem from his compositions?

Several works of Bhima Bhoi indicate that Lord Jagannāth had left Puri to become Mahimā Swāmi's first disciple

Govinda Baba, a belief that was current in the region. We need to place this belief together with perceptions of Bhima Bhoi's message among followers in the context of a crisis in the faith occasioned by the death of Mahimā Swāmi. The success and deification of Mahimā Swāmi as an incarnation of the Alekh Absolute whose *mahimā* he preached, I have indicated elsewhere, was intricately tied to notions of *Kaliyug* as a time of evil and suffering to be destroyed by the appearance of an *avatār*. The disruptions and increased exploitation produced by the colonial conquest of different parts of Odisha over the nineteenth century, the varied reactions of *gadjāt* (tributary states) rulers to the colonial presence and its repercussions on the weakening of the authority of the Rāja of Puri, the *ādyasevak* (the first servitor) of Lord Jagannāth, the devastating famine of 1866 in the coastal regions, and an increased assertion of caste and social hierarchy made notions of *Kaliyug* and suffering acutely real for large groups of downtrodden women and men. It also made them look upon Mahimā Swāmi and Bhima Bhoi as incarnations who would guide them out of a very difficult present.

The death of Mahimā Swāmi in 1875-76, therefore, came as a shock to many. Alekh *avatār* was not meant to die. *Kaliyug*, moreover, had not been brought to an end by his appearance. At the same time, the message of his outstanding devotee, Bhima Bhoi, provided hope and encouragement. It is not surprising that Dasārām, the person who inspired a group of poor and marginal women and men to embark on an impossible mission of a very long march to Puri to take out and burn the lifeless images, had received a *swapnāadesh* (dream command), a fact mentioned in police and judicial reports. The men and women who had accompanied Dasārām and were arrested and interrogated stated that they had come to Puri to destroy the idols. They also mentioned the divine command. Do we dismiss their statements, even though they were filtered by police officers and legal practitioners, as false or as superstitious claims of ignorant folk? Is it not important to probe the implications of this divine command?

If the dramatic incident of 1881 offers us entry into the worlds of the adherents of Mahimā Dharma and the remarkable ways precepts and practices of the founder and his poet-disciple were drawn up and worked out by lay followers, the appearance of *mālikas* in Bhima Bhoi's name in the 1920s and 1930s when the faith was threatened again with dissension, underscores the surfeit of meanings generated by collective recitals of Bhima Bhoi's compositions by his primarily non-literate *bhaktas*. These *bhaktas* constituted the 'interpretive community' that conferred new significance on Bhima Bhoi's *padas* (couplets/verses) at collective gatherings, attuned to the prevalent circumstances and the pressing need of the time. Drawing strength from Bhima Bhoi's message that the *Guru* would not leave his true followers, these new *mālikas*—apocryphal texts composed in the style of earlier *mālikas* that are often ascribed to the *Panchasakhās*—predicted the reappearance of the Guru in the form of Mahimā Swāmi, Kalki and Gandhi to lead the war against the British and the forces of evil. Organic combinations of distinct temporalities that blend the sacred and the secular, the religious and the political, the spoken and the written, and myth and history, these texts with no clear authorial voice bear testimony to the devotees aspirations and actions to make a difficult life bearable by taking recourse to and reconfiguring the meanings of the message of a saint-poet.

The enduring vitality of such re-articulation and working out of the teachings of Mahimā Dharma and ideas of Bhima Bhoi in the practices of householder devotees gets reflected in fragmentary evidence that couplets in the chapters 71-77 of *Stuti Chintāmaṇi* are recited by devotees to get relief from snake bite and other ailments, or in artistic expressions of Bhima Bhoi and some of his *padas*.These different practices have made the dharma and its poet retain their relevance over a century and a seven decades in a manner distinct from the evolution of an important segment of the faith as a 'sect' of Hinduism and the explorations, efforts and pronouncements of academics, enthusiasts, bureaucrats and politicians.

If *bhaktas* have understood and deployed the message and practices of Bhima Bhoi in diverse ways, scholars have examined Bhima Bhoi's works for different purposes. When I conducted my field and archival work in the early 1990s, the primacy given to Bhima Bhoi as the 'blind' tribal poet, the radical *Adivāsi* intellectual was indirectly interrogated by scholars from western Odisha who debated the fact of his blindness. They combed Bhima Bhoi's compositions and other reports to establish the 'true facts' of his life and counter thereby Bhima Bhoi's attempted marginalisation by ascetics of Jorandā and their intellectual supporters, and the undue attention paid by scholars to 'myths and stories' abut Bhima Bhoi. While scholars such as Bhagirathi Nepak dedicated their lives to establishing Bhima Bhoi as a historical figure, others, following Nepak's lead, scrutinised the *jaṇāns* of *Stuti Chintāmaṇi* to find proof that Bhima Bhoi had eyesight.Some others again, were interested in collecting the wide range of tales and legends that circulated about Bhima Bhoi and present them to a literate public. Such discrete and varied efforts, intended to give visibility and legitimacy to Bhima Bhoi the person and the poet-philosopher, had not ruled out the indeterminacy that characterised Bhima. Such efforts were also very different from the valorisation of Bhima Bhoi as the **Ā**div**ā**si intellectual, the voice of tribal Odisha, the radical national-poet and the pride of Odisha in histories of Odia literature in Odia and English published over the course of the twentieth century. Arguably, these different efforts placed Bhima Bhoi within the parameters of a historical account and institutionalised him in certain ways. But their multiple understandings revealed different aspects of Bhima Bhoi.

Bhima Bhoi in academic institutions :

The establishment of Bhima Bhoi Chairs at the KISS and Gangadhar Meher University represents in a way the culmination of efforts underway since the last century to grant legitimacy to Bhima Bhoi as an inspiring poet, and an intellectual and spiritual leader whose life and works deserve to be circulated in the formal academic arena. Here, the questions I had begun the lecture will become crucial. How do we approach Bhima Bhoi, what do we learn from him, and how do present his voice, actions, and texts to readers? What are the questions that guide our intellectual curiosity, and how do we learn what we learn?

My interest in Odisha and Mahim**ā** Dharma as a young doctoral student had stemmed from an urge to get access to and learn from life-worlds of marginal, subordinate groups of people, and in particular how their belief in a radical preceptor and his teachings allowed them to cope with, resist and subvert domination. A mention of the 'attack' on the temple in Anncharlott

Eschmann's essay in *The Cult of Jagannāth and the Regional Tradition of Orissa* had drawn me to Mahimā Dharma. In the course of my doctoral research spread over five years (that subsequently turned into decades) I gradually learnt to erase my own concerns and truly open myself to the voices and see the actions of householder devotees scattered all over Odisha as well as that of the distinct groups of renouncers in Jorandā and in the *Āshrams* and *tungis* of western Odisha through the logic of their comprehensions of their faith as they got worked out in their daily lives. It was a difficult yet truly enriching learning experience. My own understanding of the faith and its followers, that had begun with a thorough reading of archival sources and secondary literature accompanied by learning Odia and reading some of Bhima Bhoi's texts, changed in the course of my long conversations with female and male *bhaktas*, sannyāsis and participation in ceremonies of the faith. I learnt that social worlds are chaotic, that resistance is never pure, that subjects often act in contradictory ways depending upon circumstances and constraints, and that Bhima Bhoi and Mahimā Swāmi spoke in different voices that conveyed different meanings to different groups of followers.

It is this lesson learnt from historical-ethnographic research that I wish to share with you. The task for all of us and the younger generation in particular is to be respectful to our subjects—be they Bhima Bhoi the person, his compositions or his *bhaktas* and admirers—by not beginning with our preconceived ideas and expectations, and by desisting from imposing our own concerns on our subject-actors. That will open new vistas and generate knowledge that is not derivative or repetitive but challenging and incisive.

REFERENCES :

1. From the Tehsildar of Angul to the Commissioner of Orissa Division, Cuttack, 12 August 1881, Board of Revenue Document No. 443, OSA, Bhubaneswar; Jagannath Temple Correspondence, Part VI, 1880–84, No. 131, R.R., Board of Revenue, Cuttack; C. E. Buckland, *Bengal under the Lieutenant Governors* (Calcutta, K Bose, 1902), vol. II, p. 735. The records housed in the Borad f Revenue had since then been transferred t the Odisha State Archives.
2. *Utkal Deepikā*, 19 November 1881, Part 16, No. 46, cited in Devendra Kumar Dash, 'Bhima Bhoi o Mahimā Dharma', *Eshana*, 34, June 1997, pp. 120–52.
3. *Utkal Deepikā*, 19 November 1881.
4. *Indian Report of the Orissa Baptist Mission for 1881–82*, BMS Archives, Angus Library, Regent's Park College, Oxford, p. 48. I have been very fortunate to be the only one who could track down and go through the reports.
5. Indian Report of the Orissa Baptist Mission for 1887–88, Angus Library, BMS archives, Regent's Park College, Oxford, p. 46.
6. Cited in Debendra Kumar Dash, 'Bhima Bhoi O Mahimā Dharma', *Eshanā* 34 (June 1997), pp. 120–52.
7. N:N. Vasu, *The Modern Buddhism and its Followers in Orissa*, Calcutta, U.N. Bhattacharya, 1911, p. 164.
8. B. C. Mazumdar, *Sonepur in the Sambalpur Tract*, Calcutta, A.C. Sarkar, 1911, Appendix iv, pp. 126–36.
9. IshitaBanerjee-Dube, *Religion, Law and Power: Tales of Time in Eastern India, 1860-2000*, London, AnthemPress, 2007.

10. For a suggestivediscussion of these issues, see Roger Chartier, *Forms and Meanings: Texts, Performances, and Audiencesfrom Codex to Computer*, Philadelphia, University of Pennsylvnia Press, 1995.
11. See, for instance, B. Nepak, *Bhima Bhoi. Chintā, Chetanā O Jibana* (Bhubaneswar, Publication Committee, 1973); B. Nepak, *Bhima Bhoi Ātma-parichiti O Anyānya Prasanga* (Bhubaneswar, Publication Committee, 1981); B. Nepak, *Bhima Bhoi: His Life and Works* (Lacchipur, Bhima Bhoi Sānskrutik Sansad, 1998); Devendra Kumar Dash, 'Bhima Bhoi O Mahimā Dharma', *Eshanā*, pp. 122–52.);
12. See, for instance, the works of Ụdhhab Nayak.
13. Ramesh Samantarai, 'Bhima Bhoi', *Saptarshi*, Vol. 2, number 4 (1973), pp. 2-17; Rashbihari Das, *Sriguru Mahātmya.*

•

Bhima Bhoi : Humanism and World Peace

Dhaneswar Sahoo

Basically Bhima Bhoi was a poet and propounded of a religious cult called Mahimā Dharma. He came from a marginalized tribal family and lived in a remote village of Odisha. Historians give different views regarding his year of birth, parentage and blindness. As there is no recorded evidence about his birth, it is presumed that he was born sometimes within 1846 to 1855, but it is known that he breathed his last in 1895 at Khaliāpali Āshram of Sonepur district. He was brought up and nurtured by a Kandha couple Danā̆r Bhoi and Maharagi. Historians give different opinions whether Bhima was their biological son or the Kandha couple got him as an abandended baby and nourished him as their son as they were issueless. Further there is difference of opinion on the issue whether he was born blind or lost his vision at a later stage or claims to be blind in a metaphorical sense. Bhima is treated as a saint-poet though he was a married person and was not a Sanyāsi. Moreover he had no formal education though he had the scope to know the Purāṇas and some of the Hindu Scriptures in his village. Despite all these odds Bhima's poetic talent and innate creativity gradually blossomed and he became one of the great architects of lyrical and metaphysical poetry. Ironically no work of his was published during his life time. Much after his death his writings were collected and gradually printed and he came to light. Recently different research chairs have been opened in different academic institutions and universities of Odisha and researches are undertaken on his contribution.

Gradually some notable works have been published on him and his important works are translated into different Indian languages including English.

According to Bhima's own confession that after his contact and meeting with his master Mahimā Swāmi, the founder of Mahimā Dharma, his creative talent blossomed by the grace of his Guru. Mahimā Swāmi preached religion to the people orally and has left no literature on the cult to his credit. One the contrary Bhima preached the religious doctrines of Mahimā Dharma through his writings. He has described the metaphysical doctrines of Mahimā Dharma and has become very popular because of hundreds of singable devotional poems that incite spiritual emotion among the singer and the public. Thus Bhima Bhoi occupies a very respectable position in this cult. Besides, his creative contribution to Odia poetry has given him a notable position in the history of Odia literature.

Like any other religion Mahimā Dharma has a historical origin. Mahimā Dharma opened a new horizon to usher in a cultural renaissance and played a vital role to bring social reform. In the second half of the 19th Century, Odisha was under British colonialism and there were many princely states in Odisha as well. Because of famine and natural calamities at intervals Odisha was a very poor state. Poverty, illiteracy, blind beliefs, practice of untouchability, social division of the basic of caste hierarchy etc. were rampant in the social life of Odisha. Odisha was in a state of decadence. Mahimā Dhrma in such a state of affairs opened some new vista for a cultural renaissance. Mahimā Dharma was against untouchability and opposed social division of people on the basis of caste system. So people belonging to the lower strata of the society were attracted to embrance this religion. Mahimā Dharma became popular among the marginalized communities. Further this cult was against any idol worship and animal sacrifice. The idols of the various deities are man-made statues and are lifeless. It is foolish to worship these idols with funfair and rituals. In no way it helps the people. Mahimā Dharma advocates monotheism and takes Mahimā Alekha, the God, as the absolute reality. Absolute reality is the supreme designer and the governor of the universe. All are equal before Mahimā Alekha and any social discrimination is immoral. As a monotheistic religion it is opposed to idol worship, caste discrimination and meaningless rituals usually practiced by the Hindus.

Bhima Bhoi as a poet was a great creative artist. Despite the fact that he had no schooling nor scope for study, poetry spontaneously flowed from his mouth. There are hundreds of verses, devotional songs, poems with metaphysical implication, prayers etc. which are to his credit. Literary creativity can be manifested in various forms such as poetry, novel, play, short story, essay etc. Bhima has not made any contribution to prose and all his writings are in the field of poetry. Poetry, as is believed, is the artistic expression of human emotions and feelings expressed in some rhythmic way. Poet use similies, images, metaphors, symbols etc. to express deep meanings and emotions. A good poem expresses some lofty imagination and pleasing emotion by its artistic cadence. The language of poetry is emotive and its utterances create agreeable feelings. Bhima Bhoi's poetry is deeply influenced by his religious beliefs and glamour that create sense of devotion in the reader. Bhima Bhoi's poetry very much appeals to the believers and readers and create sense of devotional emotion.

Further there is fusion of religious beliefs and metaphysical notions in the poetry of Bhima Bhoi Even his religious faith and some theological doctrines get primacy in his poetic vision. A sense of devotion and religious emotion dominates his poetic imagination and creation. His sense of devotion also predominates his poetic expressions. He conceives God as Mahimā Alekha which according to him can not be determined or described. He takes Mahimā as *Śūnya* in the sense that it is devoid of any characteristic or attribute. He takes poetry as the medium to express his metaphysical and religious notions. .In his magnum opus "Stūti Chintāmaṇi" as well as "*Brahma Nirupaṇa Gitā*" he sings the glory of Mahimā, the ultimate reality as the *causa sui* or ultimate cause of this wonderful universe. Mahimā, God, ultimate reality, *Śūnya Brahma* etc. are synonymously used by Bhima Bhoi. Mahimā is the ex-nihilo creator of the world and all the individual souls or jeevas in the world. Still he calls Mahimā as *Śūnya* or Alekha in the sense that Mahimā cannot be empirically determined or described. *Mahimā* as *śūnya* is devoid of any form, attribute or description.. The multiple individual souls or jeevas remain separate after being created for temporary periods till they merge in *Mahimā* by having the spiritual realization that *Mahimā* is the ultimate Absolute Reality. These are all metaphysical speculations or imagination of a devout believer. Bhima Bhoi expresses his speculative beliefs and imaginations is poetic language The metaphysical doctrines of Mahimā dharma and the speculative imaginations of a God- intoxicated pious and fervent believer get intermixed in his poetry. There is fusion of devotion and speculation in the poetic expression of Bhima Bhoi. With a religious bent of mind he believes that the *summum bounm* of life lies in the elevation of the soul to achieve the sublime bliss. Such a state is achievable by surrender, devotion and consecration to the Almighty Alekha. One will be worthy of divine grace by unmixed devotion and sincere consecration. In numerous poems Bhima Bhoi sings the glory of *Mahimā Alekha*, the Lord of the cosmos and expresses devotion to attain a state of bliss.

Bhima Bhoi's poetic vision is not limited or confined to devotion, *summum bonum* and glory of the Lord. He is a great humanist with a humanitarian vision of life. He feels perturbed to see human misery, suffering, anguish and grief. His heart bleeds to witness man-made injustice, evil and cruelty. He appeals to God to remove human predicaments and annihilate all the evils that is wide-spread in human society. Though he was not aware of the humanist movements of the West, still he was a humanist *par excellence*. Humanists in all cultures and in all ages aspire for a just, humane and ideal society free from man-perpetrated evil and injustice.

Historically speaking humanism as an ideology and philosophy took root during the European renaissance and enlightenment. Humanists give a message that humanism is not that what divides man but what unites humanity. Humanism can be of diverse types, but all of them can be brought under two broad categories such as religious humanism and non-religious or secular humanism. Religious humanists adhere to the notion that service to man is service to God. With this belief they serve the suffering people. When people of a region are suffering or are in a state of misery some humanists out of piety come forward to mitigate their sufferings by rendering some service to them. This form of humanism is usually called humanitarianism. But humanism can be secular and non-religious as well. History stands witness to the fact that there are many crusades and holy wars for religious reasons. the very notion of humanism conveys our sensitiveness to other's suffering. In the past in religious framework people believed that human suffering, misery or predicament – may it be due to whatever reasons – is man's destiny. Human sufferings are predetermined. When countless people suffer or die due to some natural calamity or epidemic, people take it as divine punishment or wrath of God on account of man's sin. This kind of attitude or belief usually springs from a theistic mindset of the people who take God as the supreme designer and controller of all that happens in the world. Secular humanists believe that human suffering is due to social reasons and not due to any destiny. Man with his knowledge of science has been able to remove many epidemics or at least has controlled them. So also man is not feeling helpless when there is some adverse situation but exploring means and mechanism to combat a natural calamity. Man's innovative ability, inquisitiveness, rational pursuit and scientific guest have helped him in his journey from primitivism to the present age of technological sophistication. In this process man has been able to over come many a natural obstacle. Mankind has achieved capacity to enhance material wealth helping him to live comfortably. The average life span of man in almost all countries has considerably increased. Today man has been able to live comfortably which was not possible at any time in the world in the past. Famine, starvation death, mass casuality due to epidemic etc. were causing miserable plight to a large section of the populace in the past. All these things have been controlled or wiped out to a large extent. Sense of fear, insecurity, uncertainty of life and diffidence were wide spread in human society. Gradually with the advancement of knowledge, some control over nature and security of life man has been strengthened to overcome many of the obstacles and hardships. All these progresses and advancements have helped mankind to muster courage and conviction to fight against natural adversities.

Secular humanists usually do not accept any supernatural power or the ideas of disembodied existence unlike the religious people Secular humanists hold that God is a concept and does not denote any being. So God has nothing to do or has no role in human affairs. Man's journey from barbarism, primitivism and nomadic life to the present age of civilized life has been on account of human effort through thousands of years. But ironically war, violence, exploitation, social segregation, racial hatred etc have been there in human society from the beginning of human civilization. In the course of civilizational progress humanistic values have evolved in human society. It is a fact that we live in a world of diversity, variation and multiplicity On account of this some sort of bitterness, enemity, opposition and antagonism has developed among different peoples across the world. Race, religion, nationality, cultural diversity, caste discrimination have divided people and the world has witnessed many bloody battles and enemity in the past. In the present scenario man has acquired the ability to destroy the world and the whole of mankind if there is an atomic warfare for some reason or other. Under this situation humanists across the world want to develop humanistic values in all spheres of society and the world at large. Secular humanism embraces democratic values, peaceful settlement of any conflict or discord, promotion of human rights, warmth of love and friendship in the world. By this there will be more of contentment and less of suffering or unhappiness. By human effort violence can be minimized in the world. Man can shape his destiny and the destiny of future generations by his concreted efforts and endeavour. Communalism, Caste-mindedness, competition for creating weapons of mass destruction and racial hatred are the greatest evils and the bane of humanistic ideals. Similarly imperialism, fundamentalism, terrorism and fierce nationalism are taboos on secular humanism. It is heartening to note in this regard that after the Second World War different international organizations including United Nations have been trying to promote international mind and cosmopolitan outlook in the world through various programmes and institutions. Modern science and technology has made man more capable and would be of great helps to combat natural calamities and obstacles. If all forms of hatred, violence, intolerance and abominations will be annihilated or controlled a happier era of peace and prosperity will come in the world.

Promotion of humanistic values is a *sine qua non* for a peaceful world. If we want to live in a peaceful world, the menace of war and many of the socio-economic evils should be eliminated. In the twenty first century war is unwinnable as it will bring devastation to all. Under the present compulsion man has to build a value system so as to build a peaceful human society. Peace is the greatest asset of life either for the individual or for the whole of mankind. We want peace of mind, peace in the family, peace in the society, peace in the nation and peace in the world at large. Quest for peace is the creative urge in life so as to establish happiness, love, friendliness, brotherhood, cooperation, harmony and so on in the world. In human civilization despite all our material achievements, explosion of knowledge, tremendous progress in science and technology and global institutions, there are many negative dividends that have dehumanized man. Human society has never been free from conflict, discord, hostility and war. But as rational beings we can solve our conflicts peacefully and amicably. To live peacefully and cooperatively is the meaningful way to survive as rational being. Sense of intolerance, deterrence and avenge leads to cruelty and dehumanization. So also wars give rise to hatred, cruelty, to kill or to be killed and in sanity in human society. On the contrary, the moral principle of 'live and let live' is the nobler value for a peaceful society. This philosophy can remove all tragic plights of mankind and the madness to acquire atomic power in the contemporary world. The curse of war, violence, cruelty, terrorism and intolerance are the dark aspects of civilization which dehumanizes human society. Some organizations and institutes working in the global spheres are advocating for disarmament and arms regulations in the world. They are trying to spread humanistic and moral sanity not to use science for destructive purposes. Human society cannot leave science and cannot go back to pre-scientific era. But it is our moral responsibility no to misuse science for the destruction of human civilization and this marvellous world. We have to live peacefully in a non-violent world otherwise humanity is likely to perish. The two world wars in the twentieth century have brought untold sorrow and suffering to mankind. If humanity is to survive, the scourge of war must be ended from the world. This has been the mission of some peace organizations and the United Nations. If peace is to prevail in human society, then we have to create a warless world. the concept of war-free world is a notion of present day civilization. the past notions or war and patriotism should be replaced by humanism and sympathy for the whole of mankind.

Apart from the possibility of a nuclear war there are also other situations which bring threat to human existence and civilization. Industrialization and technological developments are also destroying civilization. Environmentalists opine, the ecological balance of the natural world. Maintaining natural balance and preserving the environment is also our moral duty. In the present scenario water resources, soil and air are getting polluted day by day which is another great hurdle to human society. Deforestation, limitless urbanization and burning of fossil fuel also add to human predicament. Besides, in most of the third world countries, millions of people are suffering from poverty and are forced to live in miserable plight. In India the marginalized people, particularly the *Dalits*, are forced to live a life of indignity. By their birth and caste identity they have become victim of unjust and uncaring society. Pernicious practices of bonded labour, trafficking and exploitation add to the misery of millions of people. All these practices and systems stand on the way of a peaceful society.

The idea of peace, in context of the world, consists in a war-free world and humanistic concern for human welfare and justice. Humanists give emphasis how human beings will be more kind, compassionate, humane and sensitive towards their fellow beings. In contemporary world there should be more attention by the world community of nations how to check environmental pollution, global warming, contamination of water sources and excessive deforestation. The conducive conditions which have helped human beings to evolve, survive and build civilizations must not be destroyed. In the human society injustice, man-perpetrated evil and social discrimination should be annihilated. ll these factors add to human misery and human suffering. Where misery, suffering, cruelty, inhuman attitude and ignorance will prevail, there ca not be peace in society. To love in a peaceful society and to promote peace in the world the first nd formost condition would be fostering moral self-discipline in all spheres of social life. Collective conscience, creative cooperation, sympathetic attitude, sensitiveity towards human suffering and aesthetic attitude towards justice and morality need to be developed to have peace in the world. the system of education should give emphasis how to inculcate these values in the child renso as to promote peace in the word It is an irony that despite all our innovations advancements and material achievements we have not made human beings more kind and compassionate. So we need introspection how to have happiness and peaceful living.

Today we live in a more complicated and globalised world. In a globalised world there is growing interdependence. The geographical, cultural and social boundaries are fast vanishing and a culture of oneness of human kind is growing. Under this situation human predicament and eroson of values anywhere in the world draw the attention of the world community. Humanists in all cultures and through out the world express concern to mitigate human suffering. Bhima Bhoi lived in 19th century in a remote village and that too in a poor tribal family. Still he was a great religious humanist. He had no scope of exposure to the outside world. Still he possessed a humane heart who could feel the suffering of the people. His sympathetic and sensitive attitude towards human sufferings is commendable. This feeling of empathy and concern for others have made him a universal human. Though he lived a life of persecution and misery, his poetry reverberates with empathy and kindness for the suffering in the world. His poetry also reflects his deep anguish. As a pious believer he prays God to mitigate human suffering, misery and all that is evil in the world. His thought is universal. His oftquoted stanza speaks a lot about his concern for human welfare and good. I conclude this paper with that stanza –

> *"Oh Lord! it is unbearable to see the immense suffering of the human beings and all other creatures in the world. Let my life be in hell in lieu of saving the world from suffering and misery."*

His works indeed, reflect his humanistic vision of life and concern for world peace.

•

Bhima Bhoi : The propagator of Jñāna Miśrā Bhakti

Harischandra Sahoo

Introduction :

The concept of *bhakti* occupies a central place in Indian literature. *Bhakti* has been defined as a mode of self –realization. It is self-knowledge (*Sva Svarupa*), a kind of investigation to know one's own being. Some consider *bhakti* to be one's attachment towards a personal God. In the *Rig Veda* the devotee prays with emotional attachment to the highest reality (*parameswara*) to mitigate his past vices and to grant him the desired object. In the Upaniṣads, *bhakti* has been used with emotional undertone. In the *Swetā-Swatar Upaniṣad,* the highest reality (*parameswar*) has been offered prayers for the attainment of god-head and the realization of the same. In the Bhagbat Gitā, while emphasing on *bhakti*, Lord Krishna says that the devotee is considered to be closer to Him who concentrates on Him whole-hearteldly and prays single mindedly. In the *Nārada Bhakti Sutra* and other classical literature, *bhakti* is given a higher status in comparison to *Karma* and *Jñāna*. Āchārya Sankara of Advaita Vedānta has propagated *Jñāna* as highest means for salvation whereas the *Bhabat Gitā* advocates *karma, jñāna* and *bhkati* as the paths leading to liberation. The followers of Santha tradition like Kabir, Nānak, Dādu, Tukārām, Mirā Bāi, Sri Chaitanya and Bhima Bhoi etc. accord *bhakti mārga* that elevates man to a status of higher spiritual level.

Saint-poet Bhima Bhoi was born in Western Odisha in late 19th century. He propagated Mahimā Dharma by the instruction of his *Guru* Mahimā Swāmi by composing poems (*bhajans, Jaṇānas* and *chautisās*). He could touch the hearts of lower middle class and poor people by his songs. He has composed poems in vernacular language. In what follows, we will discuss how for Bhima Bhoi *bhakti mārga* is a means to reach the godhead.

Role of Bhakti :

Although Bhima Bhoi has advocated in favour *bhakti* (unconditional self-surrender) as a higher status, he has not undeterminded the role of *jñāna* for *bhakti*. Rather, for Bhima, the devotee who considers *bhakti* as simple and easier path is totally misled. The devotee should note that *bhakti* involves a hard-core *sādhanā* (rigorus practices) for controlling his evil impulses and bad-habits. He should have the capacity to controle and regulate his own actions. His actions should be chanalised for the betterment of others. (*Paropa Kārāya Swargāya*)

Now, it is pertinent to ask, if *jñāna* and *karma* are not capable to provide to realize the highest state (*brahmānubhuti / brahmasākhyātkār*), how could it be possible to have this highest state? Bhima Bhoi reminds us that without *bhakti*, right knowledge (*sadjñāna*) is not possible. He writes :

"Binā bhaktire (he), prāpata nuhai sadjñāna
e durlabha tanu, guru sevā binu
bartiba samsāre, keun jana. (*Bhajanmālā* -16)

He says "Right knowledge (*sadjñāna*) is not possible without *bhakti*. Human body is rare (among all creatures) on the earth. Only by serving at the lotus feet of the *guru*, one can be free from the worldly bondage."

Search for a Real Guru :

A *guru* plays a vital role in this regard. Again and again, Bhima reminds us that a *Sadguru* is not an ordinary teacher. He is a true *guru* in the sense, that he is a *tattwadrastā*; who has the vision of the Reality. He is capable of taking one from darkness to light due to the Highest knowledge he has already received. The dawn of knowledge of the reality dispels the darkness of ignorance. It is not easy to get such a teacher. Such a teacher is unique and rare. Bhima instructs to findout such a *guru* who becomes the path-finder and is capable of removing ignorance from the mind of the disciple. In this connection Bhima says :

Chāri Sāhastra Veda Nāhi Sri Gurupāda
Sadgurunku Khoja Vedare ki Kārjya.

(*Bhajanamālā* – 302)

(unless you find out a real *guru*, the reading of four *vedas* are of no use)

Thus, Bhima advises us to seek after a true *guru* (*Sadguru*) who helps the disciple to remove all illusions *(māyā)* and attachment *(Moha)* form the world (*samsāra*) and to get eternal happiness. It is by the wisdom of the teacher, the disciple gets illuminated and within a very short span of time, he is capable of attaining the spiritual knowledge .

In the Bhagbat Gitā, it is said that he who has the *Brahmānubhuti* (experience of the Supreme Reality), one can aspire *sadjñāna* from him only. It is further stated that one should seek advice from the real *Guru* who is a person with indepth knowledge (*parāvidyā*). By laying postrate at his feet, asking questions and by serving him, one can have *sadjñāna*.

The writings of Bhima Bhoi revcals that Bhima was influenced by tradition (*Guru-Sisya Paramparā*) and placed *guru* in high esteem. He has accepted Mahimā Swāmi as his *guru*. In a religious congregation in Khuntuni near Athagarh, before Mahimā Sāami, Bhima dedicated his first *bhajan* to his *guru* which follows.

"Bandanā pāda padmaku
Dhyāyi Arupānandanku
Dhyāyi Swāmi Payaraku" (*Bhajanamālā* – 1)

(1 postrate before your lotus feet, I pray to you. *Arupānanda* (formless) and you are my master (*guru*).

Bhima has treated Mahimā Swāmi, as his *guru* not as a spiritual mentor but as the saviour of all creatures of the world. He could write poems due to grace of his *guru*. That *Guru* is beyond description. Bhima says :

Śunnya Mandire bihāra
Rupa rekha nāhi jāra. (*Śtuti Chintāmaṇi*)

(You are formless, Oh Lord, you reside in the temple of viod. *Niskāma Bhakti* is self-surrender to the highest being and expectation of moral perfection. The path of devotion (*bhakti*) propagated by Bhima is called otherwise as *Niskāma Bhakti* or *Alekha Bhakti*. It's not an easier task to have *Niskama Bhakti* (*Alekha Bhakti*) When one makes a complete self-surrender with full dedication at feet of Alekha (the Supreme Reality) due to *sraddhā* and *bhakti*. Thus *bhakti* and *sraddhā* go side by side In the Bhagabat Gita , it is mentioned :

Sraddhābam labhate jñānam.

(He who has *sraddhā*, gets true knowledge)

Bhima Bhoi correlates *sraddhā* wth *bhakti*. In his opinion, in *Bhakti-sādhanā*, there is intimate relationship between the *bhakta* and the God. God is formless (śūnya) but for the devotee, He is found everywhere in the cosmos. Such a view has striking resemblance with the philosophy of Spinoza who advocates that *God is nature* and *nature is God*. Similarly, the Brahman who is formless, *Nirākāra, Adehi, Niranjan, Alekha* is indescribable on one hand, but on the other, He is full of noble qualities. The *Nirguṇa Brahma* of *jñāna Mārga* is conceived as Alimighty, omnipresent etc. due to the thought process and *sraddhā* of the devotee. Thus the reality is formless and at the sametime he is found every-where.

Bhima says :

Keun thāre nāhi sabuthāre thānti,
Ātmajñāni bhakta ku se Dṛushya heuthānti.

(He is found nowhere but is found everywhere. He is only visible to the devotee who has knowledge of the self (*Ātmajñāna*). Thus *nāma* (name) and *Anāma* (without name) are same and inseparable.

Bhima justifies this as follows :

Charma Nayanare, Nadishe kāhāku
jñāna Nayanare dishe, dure nāhin pāse thāi.

(*Bhajanamālā* – 38)

(The Lord is not visible to the eye made of skin but is visible through the eye of wisdom).

Nāma Tattwa :

In *Bhakti Mārga, Nāmatattwa* is vital path to be followed. Although the highest reality is called *Alekha* and *Anāma*, the devotee is expected to chant the name (*nāma*) of the reality. *Nāma Tattwa* is the first and foremost step in *Bhakti mārga* by which one proceeds from *rūpa* to *arūpa* and from *Anāma* to *Nāma*. There is a synthesis of *nāma* and *anāma*. Bhima writes :

Nāmare Saraṇa Jāa
Jiba pare dayā baha
E dharmaru sāra au nāhina samsāre.

(Take refuge in Nāma, be sympathetic to *Jivas*, there is no better *dharma* than this in the world.)

Panchasakhās :

It will not be out of place to discuss about the *Pancha Sakhās* and *Vaisnavism* in Odisha who are the propagators of *Nāma Tattwa*. For South Indian Vedāntins, Āchāryas like Rāmānuja, Mādhva and Vallabha etc. *Bhakti* is given priority to *jñāna*. Later on Sri Chaitanya from Nadia Nabaweep and his disciples *Sad Goswāmis* gave emphasis on *bhakti-cult*. For Srichaitanya, *Bhakti* is superior to *jñāna*. It is the *bhakti* of Krishna of *Vrindāban* with emotional attachment (*prema bhakti*). But coming back to Utkaliya Vaisnabas more particularly the *Panchasakhās* like Jaganātha, Balarām, Achyutānanda, Yasobanta and Ananta Dāsa could not accept *Prema Bhakti* of Lord Krishna and Rādhā rather they give emphasis on *bhakti* attributed to Lord Jagannāth. For them, *jñāna* and *bhakti* are not anti-thetical rather they are complementary to each other. In *Guru Bhakti Gitā*, Achyutananda writes :

Jñāna bhedile Bhakti Pāi
Bhakti bhedile Jñāna pāi.

(By penetrating *Jñāna*, one gets *bhakti* and by penetrating *bhakti*, one gets *Jñāna*.)

The *Panchasakhās* give emphasis on *bhakti*. Their *bhakti* centres around Jagannath who is superior to any other deity including Lord Krishna. It has been stated :

"Jagannātha Je Sola Kalā
Tahun Kalāye Nandabalā.

Lord Jagannāth possesses sixteen *kalās* whereas *Nandabālā* (Krishna) has only one *kalā* out of them.)

It is interesting to note that for the *Panchasakhās*, Lord Jagannath is the Sommum Bonum of life. He has innumenrable qualities which cannot be described in mere words. So He is *Nirguṇa, Nirākāra* and *Aṇakāra Brahman*. He is ***Śūnya*** *Brahma*. Form among the *Panchasakhās* of Odisha, Balarama Dāsa identifies Krishna with Lord Jagannāth and advocates *Prema-bhakti*. The *panchasakhās* advocate *Jñānamiśṛā Bhakti* which aims at the union of *Jivātmā* with *Paramātmā*.

Bhima Bhoi while accepting Nirguṇa aspect of the reality speaks of *Jñānamiśṛā Bhakti*. Here *Jñāna* means (self-knowledge). Bhima accepts *Niṣkāma Bhakti* that includes spirituality, morality of human action. The *Niṣkāma Bhakti* as opposed to *Sakāma Bhakti* aims not at desire of something, may be desireless self-surrender. It aims at moral perfection.

Bhima Bhoi is influenced by Utkaliya Vaisnavas and advocate the concept of *Nirguṇa, Śūnya, Jñānamisrā Bhakti*. The *Alekha* is ***Śūnya*** *Purusha* and He can not be described since He is *Nirguṇa* and *Nirākāra*. It is the devotee belonging to Mahimā cult who should realise that the Reality is one and only one. He is *Alekha*. Alekha Dharma is nothing but a way of life. The devotee should have the sense of complete self-surrender before the ultimate reality. This is *samarpaṇa bhāva*. Bhima in his life realized this when he says :

Samarpideli Pāilā sarba
Bujha Nabujha Swāmi Gurudeva. (*Bhajanamālā*)

(Oh Lord! I surrender everything that is mine at your feet)

Thus one finds that by self-surrender, one merges in the Highest Reality and there is no dichotomy between *Saguṇa* and *Nirguṇa*, *Bhrutya* (servant) and *sāmanta* (Master) and *Nāma* and *Anāma*. The distinction between rich and poor, big and small is a matter of degree only.

Furthermore, Bhima Bhoi says that he who finds (God) reality in every being, he is called *Samadarshi*. When one sees presence of God in everything, the world becomes a family for him. (*Vasudhaiba Kutumbakam*)

Bhima advocates that human life is precious and ultimate aim of life is to look at welfare of all. In Bhagabat Gitā it is terms as "*Loka Samgraha*" or "*Loka Kalyāṇa*".

In the writings of Bhima Bhoi one gets the hints of *Jñānamiśrā Bhakti* which is different from *Suddha Bhakti*. The three paths like *Karma*, *Jñāna* and *Bhakti* are not different, rather they are complementary to each other. There should be harmony among them to realize the ultimate reality.

Bhima writes :

Kale Niskāma chitta, gamiba sehi patha
Hele bhrutyara bhrutya, labhiba Jñāna patha.

(Make your mind *niṣkāma*, follow that path, if your become the servant of the servant, then only you will get the path of wisdom.) Furthermore, Bhima expresses his humbleness when he says :

Nuhe sādhu santha, nuhai Pandita
Prakruta Atithi Muhim.

I am neither a saint nor a man of wisdom, I am really a guest in the universe created by *Alekha*. This shows the greatness of saint-poet Bhima Bhoi.

•

Framing Faith: Towards a Sociology of Mahimā Cult

Subhasis Sahoo
Sital Mohanty

Mahimā Dharma flourished in Odisha in 19th century. A number of cults like Ārya Samāj, Ramakrishna Mission, Bhakti Movement, Brahma Samāj and Prāthanā Samāj etc. started spreading across India. It is pertinent to ask certain questions in connection in Mahimā Dharma like :

1. What is the ideology and social aspect of Mahimā Dharma?
2. Why did they successed ?
3. Why were similar models reiterated again and again ?
4. What was the formula for their successful proliferation and transmission?

In the present paper, those issues are examined in the context of Mahimā Dharma in Odisha. In this piece of research on religious marginalities, we follow what we consider to be a more genuinely the religiosity of the wandering mendicants, which is ignored, not only in social movement studies but also in religious studies. While the philosophical (Das, 1979; Nath, 1990; Nayak, 2001, 2016; Sahoo, 2013; Patnaik, 2015; Nayak, 2017; Sahoo, 2020, 2021, 2022a, 2022b, 2022c, 2024) and historical angle has been explored , much is incomplete unless the sociological angle is not explored. In the present study, familiarity with both Mahimā cult (through field visits) and Odia language puts us in an idyllic position to be able to study this tradition in a movement framework.

The Methodological Approach & Proposed Model :

An ethnographic[1] exploration of Mahimā tradition may yield the answers to the above-raised questions. The ethnographic angle of Mahimā monks was explored based on field exploration and interaction with this live-tradition. The ethnographic fieldwork carried out between October 2019 and February 2020. During the fieldwork we spoke to the disciples of Bhima Bhoi, only then it was possible to understand how religion and social movement interact in several ways. Mahimā Dharma begins and spreads as a movement, through certain processes of recruitment, routinization and motivation. For instance, *why* a person becomes a member of Mahimā Dharma and why he/she does/doesn't choose, to remain so[2]. In-depth interviewing and life-history technique has been used with 40 *Mahimites* to understand the intricacies associated with Mahimā cult. Leclercq (1961) argues that the source materials of monastic cultures is of two kinds: (1) the written texts which have to be studied and meditated upon; and (2) the domain of religious experience through grammar and spirituality.

Using written text as data; the existing text includes a few archival materials available in Odia language to affirm the genesis of the Mahimā movement. These sources have been supplemented by field research which included a diverse task of study and interpretation. It is said that social history is a legitimate site of sociological investigation (Rao, 1984). It is further argued that social history provides us a novel basis for understanding the social reality while capturing through concentric circles by discovering the threads of connections between various circles. 'Connecting the dots' can be a useful methodology for exploring in interconnections between contradictions that we observe in the society (Giri, 2004). Roland Barthes established that everything was a narrative form and could be interpreted as such. It is this approach which allows us to engage in an analyses of the writings of a mystic, little known but important called Santha Kabi Bhima Bhoi, propagated Mahimā Dharma.

Before we conclude this section, a few points need to be highlighted about the nature of data that have gone into interpreting and analyzing: first of all, we are interested in the universalism of Mahimā Dharma. Second, alternative philosophical worldview of Mahimā Dharma is its objective. Third, the behavioural aspect of Bhima Bhoi and the institutional factors behind Bhima Bhoi as a personality. While our focus is more on the behavioural mechanism, an area that has been undermined yet; the 'ideology', the social aspect. We have used a conceptual model (tests, refutes, enlarges or modifies) of mechanism of proliferation (Patnaik, 2024) of Mahimā Dharma from a sociological perspective. Alongside field visits we have undertaken archival visits to access the original records (with the help of translations of local language Odia into English) for fine-tuning of text and discourse analysis.

The Making of Movement: Mapping Mahimā :

Early nineteenth century witnessed Mahimā Dharma or Mahimā Cult as a religious movement[3] in Odisha propounded by Bābā Mukunda Das[4], popularly known as Mahimā *Gosāin*, a dissident Vaishnavite thinker, who challenged the dogmatism of Vaishnavism and disenchantment with the Christianity, denounced idolatry and hence, highlighted the Buddhist concept of *śūnyatā*[5] (void, and the formless and non-attributive aspect of *Advaitavāda*)[6]. Mahimā Gosāin entered the scene when the colonial culture had made deeper inroads into Indian society. Demographically, the Mahimā Dharma has been predominantly the indigenous population of Odisha since 1950s (Tribal Research Bureau, 1968-69). It is believed that Mahimā *Gosāin* was the incarnation of God who descended to the world to establish the

Satya Sanātan Dharma. It is said that he was born out of *śūnya* i.e. not physically from a mother's womb. Living as a wandering ascetic for about ten years Mahimā *Gosāin* practised penance at Khandagiri, a cave-town, in Odisha and thereafter at Kapilas from 1838 to 1862, which laid the foundation of the new faith of a reformative cult in the tradition itself. This reformative cult was later known as Mahimā cult.

The religion Mahimā *Gosāin* preached is otherwise known Alekha Dharma or the Religion of the Formless God. Alekha means which is unwritten or unlettered or yet to scribe. Therefore, in Alekha Dharma, God is indescribable. It is said to be beyond the spatiality and temporality. It is devoid of duality and contradiction. According to Gilbert Murray (1925) religion represents a human capacity in terms of allegorically the abstract realities of human lives. During fieldwork, it was found that such divinity can be approached through meditation, an ascetic way of life, and certain ritual practices. Such ritual practices primarily consist of: (i) Nature worship and (ii) prayers practised by the ascetics as well as the lay persons. Alekha has become a well-known term for members of the Mahimā community, though they do not use it themselves. They have been influenced by the Buddhist concept of liberation. For them, liberation can be attained through complete surrender to the omniscient.

The adherents of Mahimā cult are variously called *Alekhanāmis, Alekhgirs, Alekhyas* and *Mahimites*. They are expected to follow both physical and moral codes of conduct. For instance, they wear distinct attire consisting of a knotted hair on head, a bag dangling to shoulder, and a palm-leaf umbrella over head, a *geruā* (saffron) robe for the body, and smearing head with dust. They collect food only from the donors, eat them from an earthen pot or leaf plates, and sleeping beneath the open sky. They perform their religious tasks and worship through *yajna* (fire rituals). They play *khanjani* (a small tambourine) and *gini* (iron bells) while singing *bhajans* (religious devotional songs).

The Mahimites appear as homogeneous in image and temperament but they, in fact, cut across various social categories. Many of them were non-brāhmins, hailing from the rural hinterland of Odisha. They also included *kandarās*, *pāṇas* and *bāuris*, as well as some *kondhs* from the hills[7]. Despite the institutionalisation of the Mahimā movement, the social base of the Mahimā movement did not remain unaltered. Indeed, as with many other cults, the hope of obtaining relief from a distressful social or moral condition is one of the two major motives for becoming a member of Mahimā cult; the other being a latent desire for magical powers, which are ceaselessly, talked about by the followers of Mahimā cult even when they are being overtly decry.

The Mahimā *sannyāsis* are not the lonely hermits; rather they belong to the monastic[8] orders, which have distinct traditions and practices. The rules of common *dharma* do not bind a *sannyāsi*, i.e., one who has renounced the mundane life. Mahimā movement aimed at the upliftment of the downtrodden, on the abolition of caste-system, on social as a part of religious practice and through the formation of a *Sat Sangha Goshti* (Spiritual Gatherings Community)[9] and weekly congregations. The *Sat Sangha Goshti* and weekly congregations, therefore, became a platform against all forms of Christian import into the region/ state. On the one hand, the rise of Mahimā cult challenged the evangelisation. On the other hand, the Mahimā cult does not recognise the caste-system of the Hindus and is severely iconoclastic. However, the Mahimites have adopted certain Hindu values (e.g. liberation, renunciation and spiritualism) without making an accompanying claim to caste status.

In due course of time, the Mahimā cult had its expansion to different parts of the then Odisha. A good number of monasteries were established in the then districts of Dhenkanal, Puri, Mayurbhanj, and Ganjam. The system of rights and relationships in the land, that provided a context for the complex interplay of the bonds of dominance and reciprocity. In such interplay one could see the reflection of the ritual and political authority of the monasteries-state nexus. At the macro level the Rājā-Monastery relationship was replicated in the then districts of Dhenkanal, Puri, Mayurbhanj, and Ganjam. In a more subtle and indirect manner, the traditional role of the *Rājā* (the ruler or the King) was inextricably linked with the fortunes of his people. For instance, Rājā Mahendra Bāhādur of Dhenkanal and *Rājā* Prataparudra of Sonepur played an important role in the spread of the Mahimā cult. He himself accepted the newly founded faith. They were influenced by the charisma of Mahimā Gosāin and the catholicity of Mahimā cult's preaching reformative ideas and outlook. The asceticism of Mahimā cult revealed not only the patronage linkages between the *Rājās* and ascetics but also regarded the *Rājās* and the ascetics as inextricably linked, and therein lay the system's legitimacy. Another type of legitimacy the *Rājās* derived from sponsoring the ascetics, ritual services, place of worship e.g. constructing the monasteries and making an endowment for the future management of monasteries which sets the *Rājās* as an *ideal* ruler. Further, the local leaders (or politics) in the rural pockets of central Odisha function through the dialect of [political] patrons in relation to ascetics and a permanent *sāanta-sebaka* (master-servant) relationship exists there in the central Odisha. Therefore, Mahimā cult offers an opportunity to throw light on Odisha's belief practices and lift the veil on the 'ascetics-raja-state complex'[10].

The Duality of Mahimā: Asceticism and Mysticism :

Asceticism is discipline and renunciation of immediate satisfactions in the interest of attaining the religious goal. The Mahimā monks are otherworldly ascetics. The term "otherworldly" refers to any means to salvation that tends to remove the religious actor from secular life. The Mahimā monks who are sworn to silence, devoted to prayer and ritual, withdrawn from the everyday concerns of other men. Mysticism, which is found virtually in all religions but is especially manifested in certain religions (e.g. Hinduism, Buddhism, Mahimāism and Taoism), tends especially toward the otherworldly. The mystic seek union with God. In order to achieve this, he/she may use music and dancing, prayer, contemplation, fasting and exposure, social isolation, special postures and bodily exercises. The physiological and introspective peculiarities of mystical states are empirical enough; what is non-empirical is the *verstehen* given to them by the religious zealot. It is be noted that the mysticism may be asspciated with inner-worldly activity. For instance, Mahimā monks seek mystical experience of the "Inner Light", yet their concern for social issues and their participation in the affairs of the world have always been great; they are inner-wordly mystics. Furthermore, the example of the Mahimā monks show that one may be otherworldly without necessarily being a mystic. Inner-worldly and other-worldly means to salvation are not mutually exclusive. They are often combined in various degrees. Moreover, either course can be pursed with unremitting thoroughness or with less demanding rigour.

Mysticism[11] is very much related to social evolution. Social evolution and mysticism have historical precedence all over the world. Mysticism was used as a political tool to unite the natives/ colonized and to promote nationalism especially during colonial times. Out of India came not just pioneering merchants, astronomers and astrologers, scientists and mathematicians, doctors and sculptors, but also the holy men and women, monks and missionaries of several indic-religious thought and devotion, Hindu and Buddhist. Mahimā movement in mid-19th century in Odisha is a classic example in the context of mysticism and social evolution. It saw the involvement of marginal communities particularly tribals and and a major out-caste following. Nevertheless, after the initial phase of movement, it 'otherised' both barbers and washer-folk. This is a major trend of the ādivāsi movements 'otherising' other marginal social groups which has a long history - a history that has often been misunderstood.

The Tenets and Traditions of Mahimā Mendicants :

The Mahimā faith does not have a religious scripture. However, a critical glance into the records available at the Jorandā Āshram reveals the tenets and traditions of Mahimā faith. They are: (1) Non-violence is the key principle of the religion. The followers must never swerve from the path of non-violence under the influence of pleasure and pains; profit or loss, honour or dishonour. (2) God is formless and all-pervasive. It is not possible to make an idol[18] of Him. He is the Supreme Being. (3) Caste-system is a great evil of the society and should be condemned. (4) Each and everybody has equal right to worship the Supreme Being. (5) There is no God except *Alekha Param Brahma* who is shapeless and formless. The universe is the creation of his *Mahimā*. (6) Offering of oblation to deceased ancestors and obsequious rites are superstitions. (7) *Mahimā Gosāin* should not be taken as an incarnation of God. (8) Utter the name of 'Alekha' and take shelter in the void. (9) Truthful and impartial holy scriptures are to be taken as scriptures of Mahimā cult. (10) All adherents of Mahimā cult should be away from the household attachments. (11) The adherents should treat the men and women of the world as their father and mother. (12) The adherents should worship the Supreme Being in the morning and evening. (13) They should not take their food after sunset. (14) The adherents are forbidden to travel together even for preaching the cult. (15) The adherents are allowed to take only cooked rice as their alms and strictly only once a day. (16) The mendicants are not expected to have any conflicting views. (17) The cult does not allow the adherents to take food from houses of a ruler, Brāhmin, barber and washerman/washerwoman; because they extort their tenants, exploit the society, attend the funerals and serve the people in defilement caused by birth and death respectively.

Describing the tenets of Mahimā Dharma, Mansingh (1962: 151) argues,

> This Mahimā or Alekha religion does not recognise the caste system of the Hindus and is severely iconoclastic. It asks people to have faith only in the one invisible power that created this world and to worship Him and Him only. It has no ceremonies, but emphasises the observance of a few simple moral principles like honesty, truthfulness, non-adultery, etc. It is remarkable also that unlike the multitude of sects in the Hindu faith it does not put a premium on asceticism, but assures its followers of the great religious merit of an honestly-lived family life.

This is to say that all the monks in our study claimed to be adhering to the aforesaid tenets. In the case of followers, it was forty percent. The study reveals that the tenets of Mahimā cult has remarkable resemblance to Buddhist epistemology while without endorsing to the blod sacrifice as an event. Therefore, many scholars see the revival of Buddhism in Odisha through a new garb of Mahimā cult (*Ibid.*). Mahimites question the existence of God/Goddesses. Instead, they worship the *śūnya*, perhaps as a substitute of God/Goddess what Professor Tandra Patnaik (2015) calls 'God as śūnya'. Ambivalence and avowed or unavowed, of course, are certainly typical traits to this new religion.

There are two dominant traditions of mendicants: *Nirguṇa/Nirākāra* and *Saguṇa/Sākāra*. While in *Nirguṇa* tradition, the dominant emotions are wonder and awe (and one feels a huge rift between 'i' and 'I') in the *Saguṇa* tradition one feels identity and affinity ('i' and 'I' often merge).

In *Nirākāra* tradition, the indescribability is epitome. Therefore it is inaccessible. It is awe and wonder. It emphasizes surrender through unintelligibility. Whereas, in *Sākāra* tradition, the person is embodied. It develops affinity, relation and emotion. Therefore, it is accessible. It emphasizes suurender through devotion.

Within this framework, *how does Nirguṇa tradition manage to be successful in transmitting ideology?* What is the mechanism that operates? Patnaik (2024b) argues that while happiness, love, eroticism, romance, affection, etc. are 'approach' emotions, awe, wonder, surprise, and incomprehension are 'avoidance' emotions. Yet, such traditions drew people together. What made this possible? The first set of emotions are closely linked to '*bhakti mārga*'. Ease of comprehension, graspability of simple concepts, seeing them in shape and embodiment have traditonally been linked to devotion. On the other hand, incomprehensibility, the key emotion in the context of disembodiment does not permit grasp ability, continuously challenge image-formation and comprehension. Intellectual rigour is called for and devotion seems to contrary such an experience.

And yet, it succeeds! Specifically, what forces operate to make the transmission of emotions and ideology successful in a context where one again and again faces incomprehension (*Rūpa Rekha Nāhi* – no shape, no form, emptybodied…)? (*Ibid.*).

The Transmission and Dissemination: Bhima Bhoi and Bardism :

Leaders are the agents of group mobilization and the architects of social organization and ideology. Bhima Bhoi, a *kondh* in origin and believed to be a blind poet[12], has been regarded as the key leader of Mahimā cult. He maintained intimate, personal, *gemeinschaft*-like relationships with the members of Mahimā cult. From the narrative of his disciples and followers, Bhoi was born between 1833 and 1835 in a tribal family of *kondh* at Gramadiha in the Redhakhol region of the then Odisha. After 1876, Bhima Bhoi moved to Khaliāpāli in Sonepur district of the then Odisha and turned Khalliāpāli into the nucleus of Mahimā cult, till his death in 1895. Later on, a tomb was erected in the memory of Bhima Bhoi at Khaliāpāli, which is considered as an important pilgrim centre of Mahimā cult even today.

Under Bhoi's leadership, the movement became more articulate and assumed popularity in the then Odisha by the end of nineteenth century. Bhoi identified the reason for the social degradation of the different marginalised groups such as the 'Harijans' (Scheduled Castes) and 'Ādivāsis' (Scheduled Tribes)[13] in Hinduism itself. Bhoi argued that Hinduism not only gave its adherents a religious identity, but also invested them with a range of other identities which were demeaning. The most obvious of these identities were that of the *shudra* and *ādivāsis*. For him, dispassionate (unemotional) idol worshipping is just deceiving and stupidity. Bhoi distinguished between the caste-system as prevailing among the Hindus and the 'caste-spirit' found in the

Odia society. Bhoi identified the root cause of caste-spirit in the vanity of human nature and often it showed itself in contempt for others. He challenged it by promoting Mahimā cult wherein he exalted the idea of self-restraint, tolerance, respect for the feelings and rights of others.

Mahimā cult under the leadership of Bhima Bhoi became quite appealing especially to the tribes as Bhoi was a *kondh* himself. Bhoi preached amelioration of caste and distinctions based on caste divisions which brought the marginalised castes to join the movement in order to escape from the grip of a religion which had subjected them to perpetual oppression. Bhoi saw the basic reason for such escapism as the apathy of the upper castes towards the condition of the lower castes and their practice of untouchability. By 1862, Bhoi's preaching offered an alternative epistemology to both Christianity and Hinduism. The doctrine of 'void' in Mahimā Dharma has undergone a transformation from a local ascetic and religious cult to the verge of becoming an institutionalised religion (Gusy, 2016). In Mahimā Dharma, the void is viewed from the 'Being' to the 'Becoming'.

His theory for reaching Supreme by meditation as articulated in *Sruti Nisheda Gitā*, the psychological and spiritual import of different *Tithas* as explained in *Nirveda Sādhanā*, the significance of *Ek-Akshyar* expressed in *Ādianta Gita*; the principles of Mahimism expounded in *Ashtakavihari Gitā* and the *Brahmanirupaṇa Gitā* are testimonies to such philosophy. The literality Bhoi presented the Mahimā philosophy in a language which was accessible to the masses. The *Chautisā Madhu Chakra* (Beehive of Poetry) is the best example in this regard.

Bhoi's *magnum opus*, *Stutichintāmaṇi*, is consisting of poetry in two thousand couplets organized in hundred chapters; one finds the critique and alternative of Brāhminical Hinduism around varied themes such as structure of myth, cosmogony, human-God relationship, man-woman relationship, compassion, piety and good conduct. The immortal lines of Bhoi's *Stutichintāmaṇi*,

Prāninka ārata dukha apramita dekhu dekhu kevā sahu,
mo jibana pachhe narke padithāu, jagata uddhāra heu.

Witnessing the plethora of plights on earth how one could bear with; let the world get redeemed at my cost.

has been emblazoned in the United Nations (UN) headquarter in different languages. It was Bhoi's *Stutichintāmaṇi*, brought the idea of humiliation in context. For Bhoi, humiliation was not only an everyday suffering but also a 'broken being'. To Bhoi, two reasons could be attributed for such human suffering: (i) the loss of spiritualism and (ii) the diffusion of social hegemony. One of his poignant expressions, for instance,

> Oh my Lord, why don't you help me? In preaching your Glory, my own reputation has been broken to pieces. For speaking of You as the Unknown One, they taunt me as a 'Christian' (i.e. a heretic) and inflict upon me untold suffering. They are enveloped with sin as with air, but denounce me if I speak to them of the religion of Truth. They say, Drive him away, drive him away! Let us see how his Master protects him! 'He is a sinner,' they say, 'do not give him shelter,' and when I preach equality they retaliate by treating me like a dog. My Lord, his is my fate wherever I go. I feel like not going anywhere henceforth. In the face of these tyrannies what shall I do?

Due to Bhoi's efforts, the philosophy of Mahimā cult transmitted through two paths: orality and literality. The former lacks any script whereas the latter is a script in itself. The orality ensures an empathetic and communal identification with what is known, whereas the literality distances the knower and therefore sets up conditions for objectivity, in the sense of personal disengagement (Ong, 1982: 17). In attempting to comprehend the cognitive depth of an oral universe what is called for is a 'hermeneutic' approach or, in the words of Geertz (1983), an interpretative attempt to somehow understand how we understand understandings of our own. Knowledge which is once conceptualised by oral traditions may soon be perished unless adequate efforts are made, for example, preserving it for posterity. The rhythmic recitation of psalms, hymns, prayers and prophecy that go by the Mahimites in their places of worship bears eloquent testimony to the indomitable oral spirit. Contrary to orality, the literality is a product of a tradition of writing, and its teaching has naturally demanded a literate cultural pedestal. The literal script became an agency for universalisation of the ideas and worldviews of Mahimā cult. Moreover, literality is indispensable than a causal factor, for the development of monastic structure and ascetic specialisation of Mahimā cult. The shift from orality to literality in within Mahimā Dharma is contingent upon ecology, social harmony, and social structure and value commitments.

The Ramification: Recruitment and Membership :

During the formative period of the Mahimā movement, its leaders advocated and allowed open recruitment to its ranks, and considerations like caste, age, and sex were deemed irrelevant to the attainment of Alekha *dikhyā* (initiation). This open and voluntary nature of a vocation followed by the members of the movement brought together all strata of society on an equal footing. The unifying theme which came to dominate the movement's ideology in all its ramifications was the concept of egalitarianism. The social groups in which the movement was anchored exhibited a pre-dominantly lower-caste social status following. Later the movement enjoyed the support of the traders and peasants, and craftsmen. The main recruiting ground for the movement was the lower castes. Many (i.e. 90 per cent) of the adherents of Mahimism in the present study belonged to lower castes, the bulk of Mahimā saints being outcastes. Bhima Bhoi's death however, marked a turning point. Factionalism emerged within the movement and there was the inevitable split between the advocates of the Mahimites. They were divided into three groups: *Kumbhipatiā, Kaṇapatiā and Āshrita*. The *Kaṇapatiās* and *Kumbhipatiās* are the regular attendants of the annual festivals held at Mahulpadā and Joranda[14].

The demise of Mukunda Das brought difficulties and strains within Mahimites which further got split into three groups: *Chhapanmurtiā, Tetis Murtiā* and *Kodie Murtiā* based on the number of *sannāyasis* (saints) in the group. The reason of such division was attributed to the clad of *Balkala* and *Kaupini*[15]. It is said that disputes often occurred between these groups. There is no hierarchical and pyramidal structure of *sannyāsi* among the *Kaupinidhāari* Mahimites. *Balkaladhaari Mahimites,* however, have three successive stages known as *Bairāgi*, *Apara Sannyāsis* and *Para Sannyāsis*. Such schisms were not existent during Mukunda Das, the founder of Mahimā cult. Later on, these were created by Biswanath Baba, another leader of Mahimā cult. Therefore, the *Kaupinadhāri* Mahimites do not accept such distinction. Since past eight decades, Bakkaladhāri and Kaupindhāri groups of Mahimā Dharma were locked in a legal scuffle over possession of Bati Mandir and Dhuni Mandir premises in the Jorandā area of Dhenkanal district (*Hindustan Times*, November 23, 2022).

The Mahimā movement relied heavily on conversion, the major avenue for gaining more members into the community. The movements' leaders directed all their efforts towards converting groups in a bid to mobilize support for the movement's cause. Leaders are the agents of group mobilization and the architects of organization and ideology. The recruitment of isolated individuals was also undertaken, although preference was exercised in favour of groups. The task of recruiting new members was entrusted to the holy city of Jorandā. The holy city of Jorandā issued 'identity cards' for the members (i.e. monks and followers) of the movement. Further, the institutionalization process got strengthened through the formation of a social network of monks and followers. In addition, the monastic education at Jorandā and publication of Bhima Bhoi literature shaped the movement

The Tumble of Mahimā Dharma :

The Mahimā movement faced a huge setback after the death of Bhima Bhoi. First, there was no propagation after Bhoi's demise. Eventually, there was a crisis of leadership to take the movement forward. Second, the conflict between two sects (*Kumbhipatiā* and *Kanapatiā*) of Mahimā Dharma. So, the schisms leading to open splits manisfested within Mahimā movement. Seemingly, the splits were due to differences in interpretation of the founder's theology or to a group's accentuating one part of Mahimā Gosāin's teaching at the expense of others (e.g. Bhima Bhoi). We argue that in any movement most of the splits were dictated by personal rivalries and struggle for power within the organisation and for the status outside the organisation. Third, there was a lack of strong representation by Bhima Bhoi's gang. Fourth, the lack of publications could be held for its spread. Fifth, localism, too, limits a movement and in the case of Mahimā movement, its territoriality both limited and restricted to ABC regions (Assam, West Bengal and Chhatisgarh). Bhoi's constituency was basically Odisha. Unlike some of India's other saints (let's say Kabir, Nānak and Tukāram) he never did put a great deal of emphasis on nationalization or internationalization. His cult was far more regionally focused than *Radhāswāmi* (Thakur Anukul Chandra) and *Brahma Kumāri* movements. But there were obvious physical limits on the degree to which his person could be accessible to the followers. Nevertheless, despite its size and complexity, the cult expresses, and is energized by, Bhima Bhoi's personal charisma followed by the ideological and socio-economic networks. Bhima Bhoi was original; not derivative personality. Sixth, the Mahimā movement had often been regarded as a reformist movement against the Jagannāth cult due to the worship of the idol in the latter. A critical analysis of the metaphysical concept of Mahimā cult reveals that it embodied the Buddhist concept of *Śūnya*, and the Vedāntic concept of impersonal Brahman. Mahimā movement is an indigenous reform movement in the religious tradition. It is autochthonous. It derives its criticism of the Hindu tradition directly from the tradition itself. For instance, Mahimā Dharma can be viewed as a subaltern [reform] movement (Dube 1999, 2001). By putting up an alternative to the hegemonic Hindu religion, Mahimā movement was, perhaps, doing a true subaltern, writing an alternative history of the people (Mahānanda, 2017). Mahimā movement involves complex practices, ritualized negotiations with the ādivāsis and outcaste population.

Although the Mahimā movement for cultural reform had its limitations, as movement for assertion against caste boundary, it can be judged to have had a considerable success. The Mahimā movement is essentially a socio-religious movement whose aim is to reconstruct society on a human basis. It wants to destroy caste root and branch. Though its ultimate aim is to destroy religion as popularly understood and practised, it is not as virulently anti-religious as is represented by the Mahimites and followers of the cult. Therefore, the Mahimā movement was marked by its own ambiguity and ambivalence. We argue that the moral ambivalence in the minds of Mahimites has been a canon of resistance of the past. The canons of resistance were used by Mahimites, which include Buddhism and *Bhakti*. But, we argue, ambivalence excels all other canons of resistance in Indian history.

Fieldwork informs us that the contemporary Mahimites pursue a varying mixture of Hindu *advaita* (monism), Buddhist 'vacuity', the later Hindu notions of *jana seva* (public service), and the Indian reformist's notions of *mānava dharma* (humanism). Such a range of ideas gives the Mahimā Dharma and its followers a large cultural base from which not only to manoeuver and refute the resistance of the traditional caste Hindu but also to introduce himself/herself to civil rights, equality, justice and social obligations attainable under the Indian versions of democracy. The cultural ideology of Bhima Bhoi, even if it has a cogent social basis, is actually given varied social reception among Odia population of Central Odisha. Our study of Bhima Bhoi's writings makes it clear that 'One World' and 'World Peace' were inherent in his philosophy of life which, too, resonated in contemporary times. In 2022, the Union Education Minister, Government of India (GoI) vouched for the inclusion of the ideas and discourses of Mahimā Dharma in University education.

The Final Word :

The Mahimā Movement in eastern Indian state of Odisha emerged in opposition to the social ethos of Brāhminism. As a social reformer, Bhima Bhoi upheld the cause of downtrodden and the poor. While grew up in a tribal society, the distance from the mainstream society and closer proximity with the nature created original thought processes in him. He had challenged not only the citadel of caste-system in order to establish new social order for the larger humankind but also questioned the existing religious tenants. The most fascinating aspect of Bhima Bhoi's life was his renunciation of the world through *sannyāsa*, which was not an abnegation of the world, or a despisal. Bhoi loved the world, symbolised through his poetry as the symbols for God.

Notes :

1. The idea of ethnography has been a natural trait in human beings e.g. story-telling.
2. The ethnography of religion brings three things into mind: (i) to promote the interdisciplinary study of religion, (ii) to explain the complexities and benefit of canons and, (iii) to show the several ways through which religion and social movements interact.
3. Sociologically speaking, religious movement refers to collectively to the broad range of religious and spiritual groups, cults and sects which have emerged in Western countries and later diffused to other parts of the world (including India).
4. Jogeswara Bābā, Dhulia Baba (the dust clad Saint) was a prominent religious leader of the nineteenth century. Bābā was a non-Brāhmin priest in the context of the Mahimā cult. As Srinivas (1966: 1-45) notes that the agents of Sanskritisation are not necessarily Brāhmins
5. The literal meaning of *śūnyatā* is emptiness. As Dallmayr (1996) argues the concept of *śūnyatā* neither refers to simply a vacuum or empty space; nor does it coincide with negation. Rather it indicates an absent-present matrix allowing conceptual distinctions to arise in first place.
6. *Advaitavāda* is a doctrine based on the idea of oneness of the Supreme Reality of the one and only one God.
7. The Pāṇas were a low caste group in Odisha. Kandarās were a labourer group somewhat higher than the pānas in the caste hierarchy. Bāauris were tribals, as were the

Kondhas, who belonged to the western hilly areas of Odisha. Maddox report (1920: 152-155) argues that Pāṇas were given their low status to their 'Dravidian' genesis. Besides, the Pāṇas are the service caste in terms of drum-beaters, who perform such ritual services for upper caste family during marriages, death anniversaries, etc. to a ritual payment *(dāna)*. For further details see, Lerche (1993).

8. The monastic organisation was a product of Buddhism and Hinduism (Ghurye, 1953).
9. *Sat Sangha Goshti* is a socio-religious association which prescribes for a community dinner i.e. a common feast for all laymen and followers who have been accepted into the monastic or *āshram* order.
10. When Bhima Bhoi emerged, at that point of time religion and power was co-existing.
11. In common parlance, mysticism is something which is difficult to understand due to three reasons: (a) incommunicable language, (b) uncommon language, and (c) language of supra-mental.
12. Archival records inform us that there has been a controversy regarding Bhima Bhoi's birth time and birth place; even whether he was blind or not. It is widely believed that Bhima Bhoi was blind, mean to say that his blindness was acquired after birth. Another version says that he lost his vision due to an attack of small-pox.
13. We use the terms 'ādivāsis' and 'tribals' interchangeably throughout this paper, however, the associated predicaments between the two terms still remains.
14. Jorandā, a monastery is located in eastern Indian state of Odisha (Dhenkanal). Jorandā is said to be a sacred geography of the ascetics. Jorandā, however, is a town whose political history is little-known; it has rarely been an important political centre, and the rise and fall of kings through its long history have no role in the tale of town's sanctity told by its own people.

15. Balkala is a bark cloth i.e. barks of a tree used as cloth. In other words, fabric made by beating the leaves and bark of a tree. Whereas Kaupini is a kind of loin cloth i.e. a narrow strip of rag worn to cover the private parts. Therefore, kaupini is a narrow strip of rag to conceal nudity by religious mendicants.

REFERENCES :

Das, B. K. (1979). *Mahimā Dharma O Dibyadrastā Bhima Bhoi*. Cuttack: J. Mohapatra and Co.

Dube, Ishita B. (1999). 'Taming Traditions: Legalities and Histories in Twentieth-Century Orissa', in G. Bhadra, G. Prakash and S. Tharu (Eds.), *Subaltern Studies X: Writing on South Asian history and Society,* New Delhi: Oxford University Press, pp. 98–125.

________________. (2001). 'Issues of Faith, Enactments of Contest: The Founding of Mahima Dharma in Nineteenth-Century Orissa', in H. Kulke and B. Schnepel (Eds.), *Jagannath Revisited: Studying Society, Religion and the State in Orissa,* Manohar: New Delhi, pp. 149–78.

Guru, G. (2009). (Ed.). *Humiliation: Claims and Context*. New Delhi: Oxford University Press.

Guzy, L. (2016). 'From non-Brāhmin priests of the goddess to ascetics of god Mahima Alekha', *Journal of the Irish Society for the Academy Study of Religions*, **3**(1): 171-185.

Mahananda, S. K. (2017). *Caste, Reality and Mediation: Articulation of Dalit Experience in Basudev Sunani's Select Writing*. New Delhi: Supriya Books.

Mahapatra, S. (1983). *Bhima Bhoi*. New Delhi: Sahitya Akademi.

Mansingh, M. (1962). *History of Oriya Literature*. (pp. 150-155). New Delhi: Sahitya Akademi.

Mohanty, A. (1950). (Ed.), *Stutichintāmaṇi*. Bhubaneswar: Utkal University.

Nath, S. (1990). *Mahima Dharamadhārā*. University of California Press.

Nayak, (2001). *The Voice of Silence: Sonepur Durbar and Indian Cultural Traditions*. Bhubaneswar: Orissa Sahitya Akademi.

Nayak, (2016). *Subaltern Voice: Bhima Bhoi: Poet of the People*. Bhubaneswar: Odisha Sahitya Akademi.

Nayak, U.C. (2017). (Ed.). *Santhakabi Bhima Bhoi Granthābali*. Cuttack: Granthamandir.

Patnaik, T. (2015). *God as Śunya*. New Delhi: D. K. Printworld.

Sahoo, K. 2013. *A Synopsis on Mahima Dharma*. Dhenkanal: Satya Mahima Dharma Dhama Parichalana Samiti, Mahima Gadi, pp. 32-41.

Sahoo, H. (2020). *The Philosophy of Bhima Bhoi and Mahimā Dharma*. Bhubaneswar: KISS-DU.

__________.(2021). *The concept of Śunya Purusha in Mahimā cult,* Journal of All Odisha Philosophy Association Vol. 8, No.1.

__________.(2022a). *Philosophical Reflections on Bhima Bhoi and Mahimā Dharma*. Bhubaneswar: KISS-DU.

__________. (2022b). *Dibyadrashtā Bhima Bhoi*. Bhubaneswar: KISS-DU.

__________. (2024). *Exploring Mahima Gāadi and Tungis in Odisha*. Bhubaneswar-KISS-DU.

Srinivas, M. N. (1966), *Social Change in Modern India*, Bombay: Allied Publishers.

•

Bhima Bhoi's Spiritual Vision and Social Aspiration in "Ādianta Gitā"

Chittaranjan Misra

"Ādianta Gitā" is a major work by the 19th centuryOdia saint poet Bhima Bhoi.Many of his collections of poetry are lost but the collections like *Brahma Nirupaṇa Gitā, Śtuti Chintāmaṇi, Astaka Bihari Gitā, Chautisā Madhu Chakra* and *Bhajanamālā* bear his spiritual vision and poetic flair. Like the *Bhagavad Gitā* he employs a dramatic form in which ideas are dispersed through dialogue. Apart from the philosophical contents the long poem contains a spirit of dissidence against social injustice and the cultural practices of the poet's time.Though all his works propagate the ideals of 'Mahimā Dharma' of his *guru Mahimā Swāmi* they attain popularity for their poetic appeal inextricably fused with a reformist zeal.

The very title '*Ādianta Gitā*' explores the beginning and end of existence. It is a song about '*ādi*'(beginning) and '*anta*'(end)of life. The mystic text tries to theorize the concept of cosmic origin in human terms. The dialogue between '*jiba*' and '*parama*' is designed to offer an explanation of the nature of reality. *Jiba* is the individual soul or living being while *parama* is the Supreme Reality or God. *Jiba* solicits *Parama* to know about self, creation and the mystery of body.The conversation reveals the paradox lying at the core of the concept of form and formless.Any matter be it an object or a living body has a form or shape but it emanates from and manifests the formless.

The first section describes formless as a pure pristine white radiance in which form seems to be posited as a shade of scarlet. Yet they are not different from each other. *Jiba* (form)seeks knowledge from *Parama* (formless) surrendering and prostrating as a devoted wife before her husband. The relationship between the individual entity and the universal spirit is poetically conceived as a marital relationship. As a result, their conversation appeals to any listener of the song as familiar despite the ambiguities arising out of the complexity of the subject matter.

The answers of the husband to different questions asked by the wife (*Jiba*)not only expresses the divine mystery of Creation but consistently builds up an educative sub text of man-woman relationship in their earthly pursuit of replication and survival. For Bhima Bhoi the Supreme being is "indescribable (*Alekha*), formless (*Arūpa*),shapeless (*Nirākāra*) and pure (*Niranjan*). According to his teachings, this supreme being resides in the void (śūnya) and can be attained through the ideals of Mahimā Swāmi." His musings on 'Śūnya' can be found in all his majorworks. Here too he imagines the two basic principles male and female as father and mother. Both are like two voids having a bodyless state. When they wanted to create, the father attained a body made of air and the mother that of water. The two metaphorical figures like wedded couple go for physical union that leads to procreation. Their union is described in detail with reference to ideals of sexual and emotional fulfilment. The prescriptive advice with reference to love making and sex life of a married couple contained in the work reminds one of *Kāmā Śūtra* of the Indian philosopher Vātsyāyana.

However, the metaphors used as poetic device reinforce the points of emphases the poet configures. For example, in the context of love making, he compares the woman's body with Goddess Laxmi and her clothes with Goddess Saraswati:

> The body of woman is Goddess Laxmi adorned with lotus
> Her cloth is the co-wife, Goddess Saraswati.
>
> (2003:3*translation mine*)

The poet's libidinous imagination pervades everywhere encompassing biology and cosmology. He refers to the *chakras* or the energy centers of the body from top to bottom, from the crown of the head to the tailbone (cowdal) and describes how they get activated in the act of lovemaking. At the same time, he heightens the description to a cosmic scale and brings together the mythical figures of Brahmā and Kāmadeva participating in God's desire for creation. The process is crystalized in the emergence of the embryo in the mother's womb.The womb is conceived as a cookpot in which the fluid of life is stirred by God using a ladle. The poet narrates in detail the stages of development of the embryo and the way it acquires major body parts. The fetus is like a fish playing in the waters of the sea.It is like the reflected image of the moon inside water.The soul of the life-form is nothing but the glow of the divine light.

The poet underscores body as a key to divine mystery. It contains all knowledge. The ten *Avatārs* of God have descended on earth taking different forms.In all the incarnations the bodily form is of primary importance. God has taken all the ten *Avatārs* like *Matsyah* (The Fish), *Kurma* (the Tortoise), *Varāha* (the Boar), *Narasimha* (the Man-lion), *Vāmana* (the Dwarf) *Parasurāma, Rāma, Balarāma, Krishna*, and *Kalki* with different forms designed for specific purposes in different ages. But He is beyond forms. The mystery of body lies in the entry and exit of the divine light into it.

Throughout the text the human anatomy is explored in consonance with the divine connotations associated with it.The openings in the body or the orifices are treated by the poet as ten doors. They are the gates the poet opens to move inside and discover the enormity of 'self' containing what we find in the outside world.Inside the body he discovers the master and the disciple dialoguing, the seven seas, the *Nāgas*, the islands including '*Jambu Dwipa*', the name used to refer to the Indian subcontinent in ancient Indian texts.The body in other words is a metaphor for all that a human being can perceive and experience. Bhima Bhoi does not persuade others through intellect or logic but appeals to their emotional intelligence through lyrical verses using simple and colloquial language. In *Ādianta Gitā* he tries to propagate the concept of *piṇḍa* (body) reflecting *brahmāṇḍa* (world).

Sitakanta Mahapatra observes: "*Ādianta Gitā* is almost a technical treatise where the secrets of the body have been sought to be explained in metaphysical terms. The *Jiva* or being is presented as the female of the species and the *Parama* or the Supreme Being as the male Lord and through an elaborate symbolism the essentials of the physical body, its ten gates, ten incarnations, seven islands, nine *ratnas* (jewels) and ten *siddhis* have been elucidated. The essential features of a devoted wife have also been described and the coming together of man and woman in sex-union has been sought to be explained in metaphysical terms. The essence of sexual activity and the relationship between man and woman are presented as parallel to what happens to the soul, the individual being in its quest for supreme deliverance by surrendering itself to the Lord." (Mahapatra:41)

Understanding the significance of body prepares one's access to wisdom.The mystery of body unravels the mystery of the universe. The poet reiterates in the poem that the purpose of *Ādianta Gitā* is to realizethe significance of body, to comprehend the essence of existence. Body is born as a result of the union between water and air. The mystery of this process is beyond our knowledge.In this context, the poet speaks about a number of Indian sages including Sanaka, Janaka, Mārkanda, Bhrigu, Kāshyapa and their spiritual achievement and limitations. For the poet all human beings are born of the single Brahman and their classification into innumerable castes veil their common identity.In Chapter Five, he equates the body with nature- forests, hills and wilderness are but this frame called body.

The major bulk of the text is devoted to offering a synoptic yet poetic recapitulation of the *Rāmāyaṇa* and the *Mahābhārata*.

The allegorical significance of different characters of the epics are stated briefly. He regards Rāmachandra as the embodiment of Truth or Brahma, Laxman as the ideal man and Rāvaṇa as wrath. He identifies Ahalyā with pride, Sitā with virtue and the hideous *Tādakā* with darkness. Similarly, he ascribes varied qualities to Gopis assigning them different names after local flowers. In a way he celebrates floral diversity of Odisha. Gopis are the consorts of Krishna known for their devotion. But each Gopi is different from the rest as regards her personal traits. The poet includes their follies and frivolities too. They metaphorically hint at the whole range of female sexuality.Their human qualities are viewed as creepers around the body. Essentially, they refer to *kāma, krodha, lobha*, and *moha* that prevent humans from liberation. In contrast Rādhā as an epitome of love and devotion has been equated with soul and *Krishna* is described as the representation of supreme being. Rādhā is *Jiva* and Krishna is *Parama*.

The stories from *Haribansha* and the *Mahābhārata* are retold exploring themes of Creation, Vishnu's incarnations of God, Krishna's life, and the *Kali Yuga*. The tenth chapter in nutshell reveals how life sprouts from the five elements like earth, water, fire, air, and space.The elements entangled like branches of a tree come to lifeframing the mind and the soul.All the conflicts and psychological battles of human life are described in terms of the *Mahābhārata* war. Body is treated as a metaphor for the battleground.

In the later part of the poem pertinent questions are raised as to the cause of depravity and decline of morality in the modern times (*Kali Yuga*). Since Kali Yuga is considered to be the fourth and final age in a cycle of Yugas yet to endthe poet seems to be concerned about social issues of his own times. *Kali Yuga* is believed to have begun with the departure of Lord Krishna.The current age we are living is called the "Age of Darkness".The poet visualizes the darkness ensuing from spiritual decline and materialism.

The sinful acts like murder, theft, adultery, child abuse, incest and lying precipitate the advent of *Avatār*.

Bhima Bhoi describes how a degenerate society is given to destructive forces fuelled by lust and sexual desire. But he is optimistic about a bright future which is in the making. He glorifies the *avatār* of Buddha whose penance, meditation, austerity, and self-discipline will save the world. But the Buddha he prophesies should not be referred to Lord Buddha, the founder of Buddhism. His Buddha is Nārāyaṇa, the formless who is there everywhere:

He is like a boy but is not a boy
He is dressed like a youth but is not clothed so.
He is *Buddha* the *Avatār* yet doesn't look like him
He is not a saint but practices meditation
He is not a wandering monk
But found everywhere on earth and in the sky.

(2003:104, Translation mine)

Suffused with air and water he can take any shape anywhere. He is the indescribable eternal being who does not have any form.He appears before a true devotee. He who tries to scrutinize or interpret his own feelings, seeks knowledge,possesses love and compassion for all life forms, transcends envy and treats all as equal can meet '*Alekh Prabhu*', the indescribable Lord. He is the Supreme Being; He is the One and only one. All gods, deities including *Brahmā, Vishnu, Shiva* can be found in the body. Bhima assigns different locations of the human body as abode of innumerable deities. Once the devotee realizes this, he is capable to find the *Niranjan Purusha*. Heart is chosen as the place where Jagannath and Laxmi reside.Inside the neck Shiva and Pārbati stay. Tongue is the site for the snake called death; teeth are the region for Mount *Meru*. Ears are the location for air. Eyes are home for the Sun and the Moon. Realization of such a configuration leads one to higher level of spirituality. This kind of metaphorical presentation chosen by the poet is an alternate way of presenting theory of self-realization to the common people. Since he was a gifted poet,he could earn popularity and his ideas mediated through a non-elitist diction received acceptance by one and all irrespective of their caste differences. Chittaranjan Das has rightly observed:

Whatever may be the place of Mahimā Dharma in the religious history of Orissa, Bhima Bhoi is always recognized as its richest gift to the Oriya literature. Far away from the selected circle of pundits, even pampered by royal patronage, there has been more than once the advent of a few literary gems who have grown to prominence even with little recognition but always elevating the people's mind with them. (Das:112)

In *Ādianta Gitā* Bhima Bhoi focusses human body as the site where both *Jiva* and *Parama* dwell. They are inseparable and no binary opposition is involved in their construction.This is also a way of shifting people's attention from idol worship and ritualistic complexities.Bhima Bhoi's departure from dominant religious practices of his time can be viewed as his social concern to elevate ethical and moral standard of his contemporary society against superstition and social injustice. His *bhajans* and *jaṇāṇas* particularly included in *Śuti Chintāmaṇi* refers to his struggle and embodies emotional appeal while displaying his maturity as a poet.

Critics suggest that Mahimā Dharma was a bridge between Hinduism and Buddhism sharing tenets from both. Some project him as a strong subaltern voice of his times. But it can be said that he had the ability to use poetry as a method of propagating the concept of Brahman or Absolute Monism. "Absolute Monism of the Upanishads constitutes the cardinal thought in Mahimā Dharma. It is also called '*Satya Sanātan Mahimā Dharma*'. The philosophical truth on which it is founded is that the ultimate reality is One and the only One; the human mind through ages has worshipped the One as manifested in many. But the true worship is, in the words of Bhima Bhoi, to come down to the stem leaving the branches" In other words, to withdraw from many to One and the only One." (Nepak 26)

In *Ādianta Gitā* the inquisition of the female partner to know about the deeper meanings of the characters and objects of the epic narratives is responded by her male counterpart. Though Bhima Bhoi represents woman as a seeker of knowledge, he maintains the supremacy of man as the owner and disseminator of knowledge. In marital relation the husband is the master and the wife is the disciple. But they equally contribute to the perpetuation of human race by coming together and embracing the challenges of *Samsāra*. He has rather tried to elevate woman's position by telling in this poem that the body of woman devours the body of man. *Shakti* has the power to swallow the universe. Bhima was not an ascetic abstaining worldly life. Yet he was revered as a saint by the followers of Mahimā cult mostly because of his amazing power of composing poetry.

References:

1. Bhoi, Bhima. *Ādianta Gitā*. Dharmagrantha Store, Cuttack. 2003.
2. Das, Chittaranjan. Mahima Dharma: "A Religious Movement of the 19th Century Orissa", *Saint Poet Bhima Bhoi: Views and Reviews*. Purna Chandra Rath Memorial Trust, Bolangir.2015.
3. Mahapatra, Sitakant. *Bhima Bhoi*. Sahitya Akademi, NewDelhi. 2017.
4. Nepak, Bhagirathi. "Mahimā Dharma, Bhima Bhoi and Biswanathbābā" *Orissa Review*. May 2005.
5. A Critical Analysis of Bhima Bhoi and the Mahimā Cult (Explorations in Indic Traditions: Theological, Ethical, and Philosophical). Edited by Nishamani Kar. Lexington Books, 2024.

   Online:https://en.wikipedia.org/wiki/Bhima_Bhoi

•

Philosophy of Bhima Bhoi and Jagannātha Dāsa

Anjali Mohapatra

The Orissan religion was enriched by the Panchasakhās, who as it appears, it assimilated that culminates in the Jagannāth cult. The *Nirguṇa Brahman* of Advaita Vedānta had a tremendous impact on Panchasakhā literature that has laid a solid foundation of the Mahimā Dharma, particularly in the thought of Bhima Bhoi. The Panchasakhās as saint-poets and poet-metaphysicians were strong exponents of Utkaliya Vaisnava dharma inspite of the influence of Gaudiya Vaisnava dharma propagated by Sri Chaitanya. In this sense, I shall try to analyze one of the Panchasakhās, i.e. Jagannātha Dāsa and the similar views found in philosophy of Bhima Bhoi. The distinct features found in both the philosophers are *nirguṇa brahman, nurguṇa upsasanā, piṇḍa brahmaṇḍa tattva*, etc. *jñāna–bhakti samuchaya, nāma-tattva*, etc. The purpose of discussing the Panchasakhās is to highlight the undercurrent of the Orissan Vaisnavism flowing through the Panchasakhās to mahimā dharma. Both Panchasakhās and Bhima Bhoi were social revolutionaries discarding caste-distinction, idol-worship, religious rituals leading to a kind of spiritual humanism. The rich heritage of Panchasakhā was carried down to Mahimā cult through Chaitanya Dasa who sings the glory of *Śūnya* or *Alekha* which became the pivotal point of the Mahimā dharma. In the words of Chaitanya Dāsa,

bolai Sanaka tumbhe pachārila jāhā,
ādi anta kahi nuhen alekhara māyā,
ichhā sukhare tāhāra mahimā vikāsai
arupa dehare tāra rupa prakāsai.

The biographcial account of Jagannātha Dāsa and Bhima Bhoi is not clearly known as the master-minds have not left anything about their lif-history for future generation. Jagannātha Dāsa as a prolific writer has authored many books. *Srimad Bhāgavata* is the *magnum opus* of Jagannātha Dāsa which standsout as a source book of philosophy, religion and ethics for the common man of Odisha down the centuries. He felt that these scriptures are inaccessible to common man. It is said that Sri Chaitanya was overwhelmed by the lucid rendering of Odiā *Bhāgavata*. Later, at the instance of Sri Chaitanya he was initiated to Vaisnava sampradāya by Balarāma Dāsa. He was more near and dear to Sri Chaitanya which made him *atibadi*; the greaer among the great in the eyes of Sri Chaitanya.

Similar is the case with the saint-poet Bhima Bhoi. He was born of poor parentage belonged to the aboriginal family known as Kandha in the western part of Odisha which was cut off from the main stream of Orissan culture. His father passed away when Bhima Bhoi was a child. The poor mother had no option but to bring up the child by any means. Inspite of all the difficulties for livelihood Bhima was in search of enlightnment even from his childhood days. The then village culture of Odisha which was fostered in Bhāgvata Tungis helped Bhima Bhoi to open his mind's eye. In fact the Odia Bhāgvata of Jgannātha Dāsa which was recited and discussed by the villagers every evening in the tungis was a great source of inspiration for Bhima Bhoi. Bhima Bhoi's poetic genius owe its origin not to his own creativity alone but by the grace of the omnipotent and omnipresent Lord known as the Mahimā Swāmi who blessed him to write *bhajanas* and other poetic works for the propogation of the basic tenets of Mahimā Dharma. The truth contained in the writings of Bhima Bhoi were definitely spontaneous expression of the poet which he received as a revelation through spiritual intuition. He could explain the intricate philosophical concepts with much ease which can be understood by the common man. His *magnum opus Stutichintāmaṇi* has arrested the mind of the metaphysician and poets of Odisha down through the ages. The other writings of Bhima Bhoi include *Bhajanamālā*, *Brahmanirupaṇa Gitā*, *Nirveda Sādhana*, *Srutinisedha Gitā*, etc.

Bhima Bhoi stands out as an independent thinker because of the novel perspective from which he reviews the past and thinks of the future. In religious sphere, he can be taken as a radicalist who is vocal about the exploitation perpetuated in the name of religion. The very tradition of idol-worship is questioned by him. He clearly says that the ultimate reality is *śūnya*. Śūnya is very significative because it does not refer to mere void but the state of reality where it eludes the comprehension of the finite mind. Śūnya refers to inadequacy of language in relation to the nature of Brahman. It is the ultimate end and beginning of everything. There cannot be anything which is beyond it or greater than it.

śūnya mahāśūnyaboli thākuti kahi
tānka uparaku āu bada nāhin kehi.

(Brahma Nirupaṇagitā iii, 54)

Though *śūnya* is *nirguṇa* and infinite but expresses itself in infinite particulars. His infinity is not least diminished as the infinite expresses itself in infinite ways. It is *purna* or completeness.

mahāśūnya se śūnya je nirguṇa sarira
ekaksara na basai base aṇāksara. (*Ibid.*, 1.57)

pūrnānanda pūrna Brahma atanti sehi
(*Bhajanamālā*, 78)

According to Jagannātha Dāsa *śūnya purusha* is indescribable. The only way to describe it is by negative predications. The nature of *śūnya purusha* is described by him as follows in Srimad Bhāgavata, XI-4.

He is unmanifest, without any activity and change. Neither subtle, nor gross, neither short nor long. Just know him to be without any determinations.

Jagannātha Dāsa says in *Tulābhiṇā* III.12

Omkāra is parama śūnya, all our activities too are śunya, all forms and fancies are śūnya.

× × ×

Even the celestial bodies like sun and moon are nothing but śūnya and also the empirical world, animate and inanimate beings is in śūnya.

Regarding *avatāra*, both Jagannātha Dāsa and Bhima Bhoi have similar veiws. Explaining the concept of *avatāra* Bhima Bhoi says that the ultimate reality, the supreme *purusha* takes the human form for the protection of the good and destruction of the wicked. Bhima says,

bhakatanka hite bije kale martye,
deekhyā abadhuta nirveda sambhuta.

(*Bhajanamālā*, 253)

Similarly in *Bhāgavata* vol. X, Jagannātha Dāsa says,

dusta nibāri santha pālu,
tu nātha parama dayālu.

According to *Bhāgvata* the *avatāra* is beyond the comprehension of ordinary intellect. The Lord assumes different forms, plays different games, sometimes with a view to set models for the ignorant folk and sometimes to satisfy the spiritual quest of devotees. In *Bhāgavata* he says,

Suṇa Rājana Bhāgavata,
e bada lokankara mata,
ehānka karma viparita
jeṇu e teja balabanta. (X, 34)

Jagannātha Dāsa says that mission of Lord Krishna was not only to eradicate evil forces but it was a spiritual mission to cleanse the human souls from different aberrations. He says in *Bhāgavata* X-34,

jāhāra nāhi rupe rekha, gopinki dele ātmasukha,
satyapurusha ātmarata āhuri achhanti Jagata.

Regarding the theory of creation, Bhima Bhoi and Jagannātha Dāsa have given a detailed exposition. According to Bhima Bhoi the whole creation is traced to the will of the divine. He says that Mahimā created the multiplicity by his will which he terms as *ichhāvihāra*.

thula rupa dhari ichhāre bihāri srujāi brahmāpuraku,
asesa rachanā samsāra sthāpanā dhai chārijugaku.

(*Bhajanamālā*, 220)

His will is due to compassion and grace but remains subservient to the will of the devotees.

ichhā bihāri karatā karuṇāhilāsa,
ki boli thāba karibi bhakta bhāve basa. (*Ibid.*, 22)

In the similar tone Jagannāth Dāsa has explained the theory of creation where he says that the Lord is the origin, destruction and sustenance of the diversity who does this for the devotees. In *Bhāgavata* he says,

srusti pālaṇa samhāraṇa
tu nātha jagata tāraṇa
tu nātha kāla rupa dharu
prakruti purusa samhāru
ebeni tora tanu jāta
prathame karanti jagata.

Both Bhima Bhoi and Jagannātha Dāsa have argued for *piṇda-brahmāṇḍa* identity or identity between world and individual body. The individual self is the microcosm and the world is macrocosm which are two aspects of the same reality. There is no difference between the two which is in *brahmāṇḍa* is already there in *Piṇḍa*. *Piṇḍa* generally means the body and the ultimate reality is present also in the body. According to both human birth is valuable. Bhima Bhoi says,

Mahimā nāmati jehu pratyakse manusya,
Durlabha janamati ate sakhyāte purusha.
(*Brahma Nirupaṇa Gitā*, VII)

He further says that though not orinarily visible, the bodiless is hiding within one's own body.

adehi dehe achhi, se je na disuchi.
(*Bhajanamālā*, II, 218)

Piṇḍa is so important that all kinds of *sādhanā* like *jñāna* and *bhakti* is possible through the body. If body is destroyed, we shall loose our mind and it shall not be possible for us to achieve Brahman. According Bhima Bhoi,

ei ghate thile achhi sabu achhi jñāna dhyāna,
asubhave thua amanare mana
e deha chhādile jñāna āu nāhin
aṇa hetu hele brahma pāibu tu kāhin.
(*Brahma Nirupaṇa Gitā,* XIV)

According to Bhima Bhoi supreme knowledge can be experienced if one controls his mind and concentrates on the reality which is hidden in the body. It is not certain whether you shall he reborn again with human body, so, it is wise to experience the ultimate reality while living with his body.

e deha chhādile janma nāhin,
kebe janma nebu hetu nāhin (*Bhajanmālā*, 99)

Jagannātha Dāsa also accepts *Piṇḍa-brahmāṇḍa tattva* and says that the existence of *brahmāṇḍa* is present in the body as one can see the presence of sun, moon and stars in the body. So, he says,

sakala dehe nārāyaṇa,
basanti anādi kāraṇa. (*S.B., XI*)

Again he says like Bhima Bhoi that human body is precious.

manusya sarira durlabha,
teṇu Govinde kara bhāva. (*Ibid.,*)

Bhima Bhoi has said that human body is the door for overcoming the worldly sufferings. He says,

dekha manusya kalebara
kebala muktira dvāra,
e deha pāi mahitale
hele taranti bhavajale. (*Ibid.*)

The identity of *Piṇḍa-brahmāṇḍa* is explained by Jagannāth Dasā. In *Artha-koili* Jagannātha Dāsa says about this intricate identity.

Koili boliṇa pārtha jivaku hi kahi,
sehi jiva muhin jāhā jāhā sarvatra atai.

Regarding the nature of *sādhanā* both Jagannātha Dāsa and Bhima Bhoi have similar views with regard to the path of *karma*, *jñāna* and *bhakti*. First, let us discuss about *karma*-doctrine. Jagannātha Dāsa says that every *karma* has effect on the human being in the form of pleasure or pain. In *Bhāgabata*, X/25 and 37 he says this.

Similarly Bhima Bhoi says that the relation between action and the reaction is irrevocable. In other words, the virtuous are rewarded and the sinner is punished.

pāpa karithile pāpaku bhunjibe
punya thile punya bhoga,
karme jāhā thiba grāhijya hoiba
apaṇā arjilā phala. *(Stutichintāmaṇi, 63)*

In *Brahma Nirupaṇa Gita* he says,

bihi karma karithile mahata ku jāe,
kukarma kariba loka jamapura jāe.

Jagannātha Dāsa accepts the essential tenets of the *karma* doctrine in consonance with the Indian tradition. He subscribes the view that as you sow so you shall reap. Lord Krishna advises his father Nanda to worship at the feet of *karma* – doctrine rather than worshipping Lord Indra. The law of *karma* alone determines the moral order.

e jiva ātmakarma gheni, gata āgata patha srami
karmare mate sukha dukha, janma maraṇa hoe dukha
karmati dukha sukha dātā, bisva samsāre valavantā

× × ×

karma bhunjatā prāṇinkara, Indra ta nuhanti thākura.

If action is to be done and performance of action leads to bondage, how to understand the view that action is a means for liberation? To resolve this paradox, both Bhma Bhoi and Jagannātha Dāsa say that if an action is done in a detached manner does not bind the individual because the agent gives up the sense of doership. The Lord is the transcendental subjectivity who is the ultimate agent of all actions. Therefore, the human being should detach himself from the desire for fruit of action and surrender all his actions before the Lord for attaining the spiritual goal. Jagannātha Dāsa says this in *Bhāgabata*, XI/20 as follows :

se bhakti muktrirakāraṇa
ebe kahibā bira suṇa,
karma phalatyāgakari
Vishnura bhāva chitte dhari.

Bhima Bhoi also says that one can experience complete non-attachment for the consequences since the action is not one's own. As the nature of ultimate reality is *niṣkāma*, the way to attain it is naturally *niṣkāma*. He points out;

niṣkāma brhmanku je āsrā kara,
āpane niskāma hua. (*Stutichintāmaṇi*, 81)

Prescribing *niṣkāma karma* he says,

kāmanaku ichhi sakāma bhajile
nāhin kichhi tahin lābha. (*Ibid.*, 91)

According to Jagannātha Dāsa *jñāna* is the spiritual knowledge. The Upanishads claim the distinction between *parāvidyā* and *aparāvidyā*. *Parāvidyā* enables us to know the nature of ultimate reality where as *aparāvidyā* is the knowledge about the world. Jagannātha Dāsa coins an excellent word '*nirmala jñāna*' for *parāvidyā*. In order to attain '*nirmala jñāna*' one has to transcend the bounds of do's (*vidhi*) and do-not's (*nishedha*) which belong to the category of *lokadharma*. So, Lord says,

vidhi nishedha ādi karma, chhādi sakala loka dharma,
pṛavrti nivṛti e beni, drusti sravaṇe anumāni,

sakala chhādi jñāna bale, bhaja tu mo pada kamale,
tu eka bhāve jebe bhābu, tebe e samsāru taribu.

(XI, 13)

The only path for *nirmala jñāna* or salvation from the chains of pleasure and *pain, pravṛti* and *nivṛti* is onepointed devotion to the Lord, where the aspirant is free from the dualities of *vidhi* and *nishedha*.

Bhima Bhoi also does not give importance to *buddhi jñāna* or intellectual knowledge. He vindicates spiritual knowledge in order to see the unseen, to know the unknown. When this is beyond the comprehension of the person having extraordinary knowledge, how can it be comprehended by person having ordinary intellect?

sujñāni janaka chittare adrusya,
kujñāniku patha disu nāhin.

The knowledge of the ultimate eludes the grasp of the finite intellect which is through categories that are finite. Those who are really established in the infinite Brahman prefer not to enter into philosphical debate or logical hairsplitting. That is why the knowledge of Brahman is expressed through utmost humility.

Jāṇibāra loke neun huanti, na karanti vedavāda,
akhaṇḍa brhmanku khaṇḍa nyāya kale ange pade paramāda
(Stutichintāmaṇi, 49)

In this characteristics colloquial idiom Bhima Bhoi is cautious enough against the so-called erudition, knowledge borne out of scripitual study devoid of spiritual experience is likely to infuse vanity. As a result Brahman remains an unattainable ideal. Alekha Brahman can only be attained by one who has the sense of absolute *śūnyatā*.

Both Bhima Bhoi and Jagannātha Dāsa give importance to *bhakti* which is the easiest path to attain spiritual perfection. According to Jagannātha Dāsa, it is difficult to resort to this path without the grace of the Lord. In this connection Jagannātha Dāsa says,

se nārayāṇa padmapāda harai visaya visāda,
se pāda jāku dayā kare, bhakti janme ta hrudare.

(XI, 04)

In *Bhāgavata* Lord says that in the path of *bhakti* one has to purify his mind, and has to meditate upon him ceaselessly and *with sraddhā*, he has to surrender all actions before him.

nirmala kari buddhi mana, mora charaṇe kari dhyāna,
pirati kari śraddhā chitte karma tu kara mora arthe.

(XI, 30)

Jagannātha Dāsa says that *bhakti* is primordial and the Lord is pleased with the intense devotion who surrenders before him with pure heart and mind. Lord himself says,

mote bhaktije karanti
nischala hoi tānka mati. (S.B. X)

Jagannātha Dāsa is for *prema-bhakti*, which is associated with the *gopi-bhāva* for the Lord Krishna, where devotee expresses his love for the Lord. Jagannātha Dāsa says;

sakti bale sangita bhajana suṇi
chitta pātre thibe kari dhari.

(Nityanilādri Vilāsa, 21 verse)

Bhima Bhoi gives supreme importance to *bhakti*. It implies an exclusive relation between the devotee and the object of love. The absolute which is an object of love is not an abstraction or a theoretical postulate but a living entity. The uniqueness of Bhima Bhoi is that although he accepts the impersonal Brahman but he reveres Brahman as Mahimā as the abode of all virtues, *rupas* and *guṇas*. He says the *Anādi* and Alekha assume a form only for the devotees.

se je anādi Alekha, honti kalebara rupa,
Bhakta hitare he. *(Bhajanmālā, 214)*

The type of *bhakti* recommended by Bhima Bhoi is *niṣkāma bhakti* or *alekha bhakti* which requires that there must be complete surrender of the aspirant, when he realizes that God is omnipotent and all-merciful. He takes refuge with unshakeble faith in the Lord for attaining his goal. He discards the idea of 'I' and 'mine' and dedicates his heart and soul to the eternal Lord.

samarpi piṇḍa prāṇa sutta bitta dhana,
dhari mote udāsina niṣkāma manare he.

(Bhajanamālā,, 32)

Bhima Bhoi glorifies *niṣkāma bhakti*. If *bhakti* is treated as a means for attaining something, even the Absolute then it is *sakāma bhakti*. If *bhakti* is treated as an end itself, i.e. *bhakti* for the sake of *bhakti* then it is *niṣkāma bhakti*. The Lord is pleased with *niṣkāma bhakti* and reveals himself before the devotee.

niṣkāma hoile mana drusya hebe parambrahma.

(Ibid., 173)

At the highest stage of *bhakti*, nothing but the absolute shines in its prestine consciousness. The Lord, or the sole object of the devotee ensures his devotees that he is constantly attached to the devotee. Lord himself says that it is very rare to get a real devotee, who is part and parcel of the Lord himself and Lord is infatuated by the unconditional devotion of the devotees. So, Lord says;

dekhi tā niṣkāma bhakti,
āmbhe na chhādu tāra kati,
× × ×
bhakata āmara prāṇahita,
teṇu tā bhāvare mohita. (Ibid.,)

In the context of *bhakti sādhana*, it is necessary to analyse the role of guru or spiritual guide. Both Bhima Bhoi and Jagannātha Dāsa accept the importance of guru for attaining self-knowledge. The aspirant must pine for the instruction of the guru who is *tattvadrastā* and is embodiment of perfection. The spiritual guide shows new horizons of spiritual upliftment of the aspirant who guards the aspirant against the pitfalls or ill dispositions. Bhima Bhoi points out the importance of guru in spiritual path by saying :

sadgurunku khoja, Vedare kisakārya.

(Bhajanamālā, 302)

Bhima Bhoi accepts Mahimā Swāmi as his guru. Bhima Bhoi surrenders himself wholeheartedly at the lotus feet of the guru who is not only the spiritual guru but also the ultimate reality. He admits that he is ignorant and his genius is attributed to the grace of guru who is Lord himself.

Sriguru krupāru mora kabi paṇa
bālakavayase buddhi nāhin mo jñāna.

(Ādianantagitā, I)

Jagannātha Dāsa who admits that guru is the Lord himself, and without the grace of guru it is not possible to overcome ignorance and miseries of the world. So, by serving guru one can attain *sādhanā* and he is gracious enough to offer *mukti* to the devotee. Jagannātha Dāsa says,

gurunku namaṇiba nara,
guruhin sakṣāt isvara. (S.B I)

There he asks to take resort to the spiritual guide who is engrossed in *Brahmavidyā* and can impart right instructions for the realization of Brahman. So he recommends,

e kathā bujhi gurupāde, āsre kariba apramāde,
uttama guru āsrā kari, tānka bachana sire dhari,
seva kariba drudhachitte, je guru sisya bhāva mate,
eṇe prasanna Nārāyaṇa karanti ātmajñāna dāna.
(Ibid.)

Indian spiritual tradition gives importance for *nāma-sādhanā* which opens the door for spiritual perfection for all. Bhima Bhoi and Jagannātha Dāsa give importance on *nāma* as the easiest path for *bhakti*. This is essential for progressing as ultimate reality is formless, who plays the role of nature of *nāma*. It is through *nāma* alone one can liberate himself from the bondage of the world. *Nāma-smaraṇa* is highly praised by Jagannātha Dāsa as *nāma* is all powerful through which *bhakti* can be attained. He says in *Bhāgabata*, 11/26.

nāmare achhi sarva sakti,
nāmare labhe hari bhakti.

The importance of *nāma-tattva* is clearly explained by Jagannātha Dāsa who says that if a devotee with intense love utters, listens and meditates on name of Lord Krishna, he overcomes all imperfections and attains the Lord.

krshna nāma japuthānti,
phitila bhava bhaya bhrānti. (X, 24)

× × ×

bhajai krshna padmapāda
svarge pāiba indrapada. (X, 41)

Bhima Bhoi though admits mahimā as a *nāma*, says that the devotee can reach the ultimate reality by uttering the *nāma* of mahimā. According to him one has to completely surrender to the *nāma* and be compassinate to all as this is the best *dharma* in the world.

nāmare saraṇa jāa, Jiva pare dayā bhāba
e dharma ru sāra nāhin nā samsāre.

(Bhajanmālā, 38)

Pointing out the importance of *nāma* he pleads again and again to all to engage in any professional work they choose but can get perfection if they uninterruptedly keep the *nāma* in their heart. Mahimā *nāma* is the best *nāma* which shows the path to become immortal.

suṇilulki nirākāra mahimānka riti
mahimā nāmati jehu jivana mukati
mahimā nāmati jehu chāri juge sāra
mahimā prakāsa hele huanti amara.

(Brahmanirupaṇagitā, VII, 57)

It is generally believed that the path of *jńāna* and *bhakti* are exclusive and opposite of each other. Bhima Bhoi and Jagannātha Dāsa propound *Jñāna-misrā bhakti* where it is pointed out that both are complementary to each other. *Bhakti* has for it object the merciful Lord and thorough knowledge of the Lord it is essential for it. If realisation of Brahman is due to a kind of spiritual knowledge, the the question is, how it can be attained? According to Bhima Bhoi *sadjńāna* is not possible without *bhakti*.

binabhaktire he prāpata nuhen sehi jñāna...
(Bhajanmālā, 16)

Bhima Bhoi clearly states that *jñāna* is not possible without the grace of God which is the gift of God that cannot be attained by study of scriputres. So, Bhima Bhoi exhorts the aspirant for the path of knowledge to pray God for fulfilling his aspirants.

jñāna ghara kathā asrsṛta avyakta
binā bhakti re ki labhibu,
to hṛudapadmaru jñāna jāta hele
tebe sinā tuhi taribu. *(Stutichintāmaṇi, 88)*

According to Jagannātha Dāsa, *Jñāna* and *bhakti* are not exclusive paths. The difference between these two paths is not real but superficial. This superficiality, if not properly understood causes sorrow and suffering. He says,

Jñāna yoga re tānkupāi
bhakti yoga re labhesehi,
kebala mārga mātrabheda
na bujhipāe labhu dukha. *(Arthakoili, 11)*

Bhakti is associated with *Jñāna*, the role of *jñāna* is explained by Jagannātha Dāsa for spiritual *sādhanā*.

mote bhajanti jñāni jana
mun tānka ista priyadhana,
je mate jñāna bandhe dhare
se sarba kāma karipāre. *(SB. II)*

It implies a deep commitment of the self to be restored in its original state. It is a loving faith that initates and sustains the *jñāna* leading to the goal. *Bhakti* has the negative function of warding off doubt or suspicion which stands on the way of total participation of the individual in the process of knowing the self. Devoid of *bhakti*, *jñāna* is mere information and devoid of *jñāna, bhakti* is mere sentimentality. So again and again the aspirant prays the almighty or the guru to shower his grace so that *jñāna* can have a significant role in overcoming the cycle of birth and death.

In the philosophy of Bhima Bhoi and Jagannātha Dāsa one discovers a unique synthesis of knowledge, action and devotion. The devotee struggles to realize the highest state by cultivation of highest knowledge and performance of right action. These three paths *jñāna, karma* and *bhakti* are not exclusive paths leading to perfection but are mutually complimentary as one sustains the other. So Panchakhā tradition serve as the backdrop which Bhima Bhoi gave expression to his philosophic conviction. So we find there is a striking similarity between Bhima Bhoi and Jagannātha Dāsa with regard to metaphysical world-view, epistemology and ethics.

Both Bhima Bhoi and Jaganātha Dāsa were spiritual humanists. Bhima Bhoi does not reject multiplicity but sees it as manifold expression of the same reality. He sees himself in everyone and everyone in himself. He says,

sakala bhutare eka atmāprāya dekhe
samastaku bole mora, muhi atai tumbhara.

Bhima Bhoi believed in spiritual humanism which does not treat man as an end in relation to non-humans who are the means. He thought beyond human species and embraced non-humans in the sweep. In *Bhajanamālā, 66* he prays to the Lord not only to save the human species but also the animals, birds, insects as these are the kindred selves and manifestation of the Lord himself.

Jagannātha Dāsa also hold the similar view. According to him the human values envisaged in the *Bhāgavata* do not mean the values pertaining to human being only. The real value consists in respecting non-humans as well. It is a vision of spiritual community where the well-being of man as well as others are to be taken care of through love and service and man being the most rationally developed ought to shoulder this responsibility. Jagannātha Dāsa gives the examples of tree who amid all turbulances goes on doing good to the environment as well as to the society. The tree is the model representative of the environment and symbol of self-less service.

•

Guru tattva and Nāma-tattva in Philosophy of Bhima Bhoi

Sarat Chandra Panigrahi

In Indian spiritual tradition the importance of *guru* is highlighted for obtaining self-knolwedge. The aspirant after attaining moral perfection it is necessary for him to go to the *guru* for his spiritual instruction. As song as he does not get *dikshyā* (initiation) from the *guru*, he cannot attain self-knowledge as *guru* has realised his identity with the supreme who transcends intellectual knowledge. Self-knowledge is not possible by one's self-effort as the absolute is not a theoretical postulate but a living entity who can be realised by the grace of the *guru*. Bhima Bhoi accepts *jñāna-misṛā bhakti*. In order to understand this form of *sādhanā* we must enquire about the role of *guru* and *nāma-tattva* as in both the concepts there is a blending of *jñāna* and *bhakti*.

The *guru*-tradition is an important part of *mahimā - sādhanā*. Hence it is necessary to analyse the role of *guru* or the spiritual guide. For Bhima Bhoi *guru* is not an ordinary teacher but he is the Lord himself. Though the intense love for the supreme is the easiest path, *guru* is necessary for obtaining self-purification as well as self-knowledge. The aspirant must pine for instruction of the *tattwadṛastā* or *guru* whose purpose is to impart highest knowledge i.e. *ātmajñāna*. The *guru* opens new horizons of spiritual upliftment of the aspirants. He also guards the aspirant against the pitfalls or perverse dispositions. The most significant aspect of a spiritual guide is that he is in the constant habit of purifying the heart of the devotee and showing him the proper direction. The duty of the aspirant is to take resort to the grace of *guru* by discarding all immoral dispositions.

Guru is supposed to be embodiment of perfection. The aspirant acquires self-knowledge by placing in the saving grace of *guru* who removes all misconceptions and ignorance that he has. In *Muṇḍaka Upanishad,* 1.2.12 the qualities of a *guru* is clearly indicated "... for the sake of knowledge let him approach a teacher who is learned in the scriptures and established in Brahman." In the Gitā, IV. 34 it is also said that we can get self-knowledge by our devotion to the *guru* who has experienced the truth.

tad viddhi praṇipātena
pariprasnena sevayā
upadekhyanti te jñānam
jñāninastattva darsināh

(Learn that by humble reverence, by inquiry and by service, the men of wisdom who have seen the truth will instruct thee in knowledge.)

Bhima Bhoi points out the importance of *guru* in spiritual path by saying,

sadguruku khoja vedare kisa kārya.

Now let us find out the views of Panchasakhās regarding nature and role of the *guru*.

Balarāma Dāsa says in *Gupta Gitā*, that by serving *guru* one can attain *sadjñāna.* In the same text he says that *guru* is *nirākāra* and the aspirant who has the highest virtue only can get such a *guru.*

guruti brahma harihara, guruti svayam nirākāra,
emanta gurunkar sevā, je prāṇi se durlabha.

In *Gurubhakti Gitā* Achuytānanda Dāsa explains in detail how *guru* is gracious enough to offer *mukti* to the devotee.

guru mukati gati dātā,
guruhin jiva uddhārantā.

Similarly, Yasovanta Dāsa says in *Ātmaparche Gitā* that without the grace of *guru* it is not possible on the part of the individual to overcome ignorance and miseries of the world.

gati mukati hi karatā guru,
guru na sebi ke samsāre taru.

Guru is the one who helps the disciple to ascend the path of *sādhanā*. He as the boat takes the disciple from the sea of suffering to the highest state and rescues him. Achyutānanda says:

e bhava samudra atai, guru tahinki nāba hoi,
uttama dharma nāma kahi, uttam janma dyanti sei.

Guru is just like a lamp, who enlightens the disciple showing the path from darkness to light. *Guru* is the one who acquaints us with *mahā Śūnya* whereby we can get everything that is desirable.

Selection of perfect *guru* is very difficult as it is very rare to find him as he knows the proper path for attaining perfection. In *Gurubhakti Gitā*, Achyutānanda says,

uttamaguru pāda sevā, bhagati patha dekhāiba,
eṇu subija guru khoja, agādi dhāne kisa kārya.

Manu has explained the inevitable role of *guru* for *sādhanā*. He is *Siddhidātā*, self-complete and destroyer of sins. Achyutānanda explained the glory of *guru* through whom spiritual knowledge is possible and the disciple gets rid of all worldly suffering.

samsāra ye mahāghara yātanā janjāla,
sadguru sevā kale nāsa hue kāla.

Balarāma Dāsa in *Gupta Gitā*, p.9 says, if there is *krupā* of *guru,* we can be rescued from the dark well of ignorance and the instruction of *guru* is a guidance for the right path in *sādhanā* for attaining spiritual knowledge.

guru jñāna upadesa tāku ye boli,
sujñāni nirmala dehi supatheṇa chali.

guru sevāre jñānapāi, andha kuparu uddhārai,
guru na sevile Arjun, kāhun pāiba sadjñāna.

So *guru* being the Lord himself becomes an instrument as the preceptor and mediator between the Lord and devotee. It is important to note here that the *guru* shows the path but the devotee by his spiritual practice has to tread the path alone leading to perfection by himself. In *Tattvabodhini*, Achyutānanda says:

āpaṇā manaku āpe dekhiba,
guru sinā bāta batāi deba.
jāhār jepari viswās thiba,
se nara separi phala bhogiba.

Ananta Dāsa emphatically says that without the worship of *guru*, the *jiva* cannot be liberated from the cycle of birth and death.

bandai sree guru charaṇa,
guru jivara paritrāṇa...

Bhima Bhoi is of the view that the *guru* has to be respected in high esteem as he is the only medium through whom *sadjñāna* can be attained. He also warns by saying that mere listening to the advices of *guru* and promising that he will follow all his instructions is not enough. He has to transform his promises into action otherwise he will deviate himself from the path of *sadjñāna*.

Bhima Bhoi accepts Mahimā Swāmi as his *guru*. For him, *guru* is not an embodied person or a human being. He is *aṇākāra*, *arupānanda*, *alekha* and *śūnya*. He confesses in the beginning that it is by the grace of *guru* he has received all the virtues of the world. He admits that he is ignorant and bereft of any creativity. His poetic genius is attributed to the grace of *guru* or the Lord. He says in *Ādianta Gitā*,

sriguru krupāru mora kavi paṇa,
bālaka vayasa buddhi nāhin mo jñāna.
guru ajñāre karichhi mo kavikrutya,
mu kisa karibāku je samartha.

Bhima Bhoi says that there is no difference between *guru* and *sisya*. He says again in *Stutichintamaṇi*.

dehare jesana charma ghodāichhi charmare ābori roma,
chāri juge kebe bhinna bhinna nuhen guru sisya eka mana.

× × ×

sarira jesana jiva paramati nuhanti se bhinna bhinna,
sei anubhave bujhāmaṇā kara guru śisyankara mana.

Guru and *sisya* are so similar that they live together and eat together. So no discrimination is admissible between them. Bhima Bhoi is explicit in this.

kehu ate guru kehu ate śisya,tahin na thāi bāraṇa.
bhakta bhagabān eka anga jāṇa ekānta thābe saraṇa.

A true *guru* is one who protects the devotee. None expect *guru* is capable of doing this arduous task of realisation of the reality. Bhima Bhoi says that since his birth he could know this,

piṇḍa prāṇa rakhyā kehi na atanti eka gurudeba binu,
medinire thāi sakala jāṇuchhi janmaheli jete dinu.

As there is no distinction between piṇḍa and brahmāṇḍa, there is no distinction between *guru* and *śisya*. He says in *Stuti Chintāmaṇi, 37,*

guru śisya duhen ekatva atanti,
antara maṇiba nāhin.

He loves devotee so much that the *guru* feels as if they are the parts of the same body. The relation is such that as devotee worships the *guru*, in a similar manner *guru* also is devoted to the *śisya*. He mentions it in *Stuti Chintāmaṇi* 68,

Bhagat angati prabhu angajāhā, jiba rūpe kari bije,
guru charaṇaku śisya bhajuthāi, sree guru śisyaku bhaje.

Devotee is worried when there is pain or suffering of the *guru*. Similarly *guru* is also concerned when devotee is in the bondage of suffering. This is mentioned in *Stuti Chintāmaṇi*, 37,

srigurunka anga byathā heuthile,
bhaktaku lāgai chintā.
bhagat dukha phāndare pasithile
sree gurunku lāge byathā.

The nature of the *guru* is such that he always wants to shower his grace on the devotee as the devotee wants the mercy of the *guru*. This organic relation is so intense that both are one and the same, therefore Bhima Bhoi says in *Stuti Chintāmaṇi* 37 that one should not think of any distinction between them :

Sree guru lodai dayā karibāku sevaka lodai dayā,
benijana tahin ekaprāṇa hoi na thāe antare māyā.

It is also significant that *nirveda* or *guru* is also the most dearest friend and saviour of the devotees. With all humility Bhima Bhoi prays for the mercy of the *guru* as described in *Stutichintamaṇi*. 38,

bahuta avasthā hoilāṇi mate ki karibi guru kuha
ki prakāre mote niārā tataparijare thua,
prabhunku na kahi kāhāku kahibi ke bujhiba mora dukha,
dukhijana bandhu ata parā tumbhe krupā kari mote rakha.

The impersonal becomes personal, the infinite becomes the finite, the indescribable assumes the human form as the *guru*. Who else can be so gracious than the *guru*? This shows how the *bhakti mārga* excels the *jñāna mārga*. The incomprehensible reality for the aspirant of *jñāna mārga* becomes the loving and personal God for the follower of *bhakti mārga*.

In *Bhajanamālā 6*, Bhima Bhoi says that though each one is potentially divine but without surrendering and serving *guru* none can rescue him from the world of suffering.

e durlabha tanu guru sevā binu,
bartiba samsāre keun jana.

Kabir also says that the importance of *guru* is so vital that by his grace the mind of the the disciple which was roaming here and there was feeling restless has become steady and enjoys calmness and bliss.

If Kabir has an option to choose between the Lord and the *guru,* he shall choose the *guru* who is the only one to show him the path leading to the attainment of the Lord. He says,

Guru Gobinda doei khade,
kāku lāgu pāya,
guru āap balihāri
jo Gobinda dio batāya.

Kabir says that *sadguru* is to be chosen who does not have greed, worldly-attachment and is bereft of all doubts. If you get *sadguru,* then all the virtuous qualities shall be endowed upon you and you can overcome all attachments for worldly objects and can have steady mind both in pleasure and pain and you become like a *guru.*

Kabir clearly says that the disciple most purify himself by cleansing his mind and surrendering before his *guru* otherwise he cannot grasp the valuable instructions of the *guru.* In this case the fault does not lie in the *guru* but in the disciple just as if a piece of cloth is dirty, the dye cannot be retained in the cloth. The fault lies with the dirty cloth not with the dye.

guru bichārā kyā kare sabad na lāge ang,
kahe Kabir maili gaji kaise lāge rang.

Guru is the person who perfects the disciple by strict discipline for removing all the blemishes and imperfections but he is kind enough to protect the devotee from all trials and tribulations he faces in the path of *sādhanā*. Kabir gives analogy of potter and pot to explain this by comparing *guru* as the potter and *śisya* as the pot. *Guru* as the potter eradicates all the imperfections by beating it from outside and protects it by holding his hand from inside.

guru kumbhāra sish kumbh hai,
gadh gadh kadhei khot
antara hāta sahāra dai,
bāhar bāhyai chot.

Bhima Bhoi admits that no evil has touched him after serving *guru* and has surrendered his *piṇḍa* when there was awakening of *buddhi* and *jñāna* in him. In *Stutichintāmaṇi*, 77 he says,

niṣkalanka heu kalanka na thāu guru sevā kalā tanu,
piṇḍa prāṇa mora samarpi deichi jñāna buddhi helā dinu.

Bhima Bhoi refers Mahimā Swāmi as he is *guru* and calls him as *gurubrahma, gurudeva Swāmi, mahimā sāgara* etc. In *Brahmanirupaṇa Gitā* he says,

Mahimā nāmati jehu atai namāmi,
sāra Brahmajñāna se sakhyāte guruswāmi.

He says that one who has dedicated himself for *guru-sevā*, attains peaceful death and *kāla* is terrorised to take him by Yama. After a thoughtful deliberation he proclaims that if anyone is not capable of performing any kind of *sādhanā*, he has just to follow *gurusevā dharma* which is the best form of *sādhanā*. In *Stutichintāmaṇi*, he declares,

mora bichāraku jāhā disuachhi gurusevā dharma sāra,
kichhi hi na kale gurusevā dharma jebe achha tebe kara.

x x x

guru sevā loka nirmala maraṇa, na jāanti yamara kati.

x x x

guru dharme jebe tattva rahithiba, nische uddhāra pāiba.

x x x

guru krupā kale e deha rahiba anyare nuhai kichhi.

Bhima Bhoi treats his *guru* in many forms. At times he treats *guru* as his father, as his son etc. Being a son of his *guru*, he asks him to get up from sleep as it is late in the morning. In *Bhajanamālā*, he says,

utha swāmi brahmāṇḍa thākura,
bije kara bela heuchhi uchhura.

He again says that *guru* is just like his son, whom he has lovingly caressed by making him sit on his lap. He expresses his feeling in the following manner in *Bhajanamālā*, 45,

bāpa dhana boli gela karuthili, basithile mora kolare

He also treats him as a guest in the world, so he is reluctant to express his suffering.

bolāa athitibesa dukha mu kahibi kisa?

Guru also treats the disciple as his father and assures him that he shall abide by the commands of his disciple. In *Stutichintāmaṇi*, 88, the *guru* says,

mu tohar putra tu mohara pitā etiki viswās nebi,
mote tuhin jahin basāibu bhakta tahin muhin basithibi.

No doubt is dispelled without the words of wisdom of the *guru*. Therefore, Bhima Bhoi says in *Brahmanirupaṇa Gitā*, 12, never to be swayed away by what you see or listen.

guru na kahile kichhi samsaya na jāe,
dekhilā suṇilā kathā aparate jāe.

Therefore, Bhima Bhoi appeals his *guru* to open the door of *sadjñāna,* quickly as it is very late. In *Bhajanamālā*, 302, he says,

dekhāa jñānabāta, phitijāu samkata,
uchhura heuchita, ājñā heu turita.

Bhima Bhoi says that without *jñāna, bhakti* is not possible. The *bhakta* must have the knowledge that *Alekha puruṣa* is the inner self of all and the entire universe is created out of him. He is immanent in all created beings. A *brahmajñāni* is devoted to the Lord spontaneously. Bhima Bhoi's comments on this important view is that it is *jñāna* which generates *bhakti* as stated in *Bhajanamālā*, 18,

kehuṇi thābare nāhin sabuthāre thānti,
ātmajñāni bhaktaku se dṛusya hoichhanti,
ekakṣara pada chinhi bhajuchhanti brahmajñāni.

The ultimate goal is realisation of absolute. In *jñāna mārga*, the subject or the *sādhaka* tries to know the ultimate reality of its infiniteness. But *bhakti mārga* gives importance on the object i.e., Infinite as the object of consciousness and there is the duality between Lord and the devotee. The devotee realizes the all-merciful nature of God, so he surrenders everything to the Lord. His surrender is prompted by his unshakable faith in the Lord as the redeemer. In *jñāna mārga* the devotee has *ātmajñāna* that reality is incomprehensible but in *bhakti*, the Lord is transmuted as loving and personal God. In *true bhakti, bhakta* forgets his own creature-consciousness and Lord also forgets his *Isvaratva* and seeks the *bhakta* as his life and love which is rare to find in three worlds. He says in *Stutichintāmaṇi*. 88,

emanta bolanti alekha purusha,
niṣkāma bhaktaku chāhin.
toha moha bhāba jebaṇa pirati,
tribhubane jaṇā nāhin.

This arises when there is absolute self-resignation to the will of God. In its highest form the devotee is not conscious of his self-surrender. When the devotee reaches through his love at the apex of the pyramid of *bhakti*, the so called distinction between *jñāna* and *bhakti*, *saguṇa* and *nirguṇa* is dissolved. Intense devotion surpasses everything and in the ultimate analysis what dazzles alone is *śūnya purusha* who assimilates and overcomes all distinctions.

From the writings of Bhima Bhoi it is quite evident that he was initiated to the *guru* tradition. In conformity with this tradition, Bhima Bhoi places his *guru* at the highest place. It is said that the first *bhajan* written by Bhima Bhoi was dedicated to his *guru*. Bhima Bhoi surrenders himself wholeheartedly at the lotus feet of the *guru* who is not only the spiritual instructor but also the ultimate reality.

In *Stutichintāmaṇi* he says that he has not learnt anything from any teacher directly. He has only prayed for the grace of *guru* and has written by the intuitive insight gifted by the *guru*. Apart from this, the poet-philosopher holds his *guru* at the highest position. For him, the Ultimate Reality or the Mahimā Swāmi is both the knowledge *per* se and the ultimate knower or the *guru*. The characteristics of the *guru* are indescribable. He says of the *guru: Śūnya mandire vihāra, rupa rekha nāhin tāra.*

The *guru* resides in the abode of the ultimate void having no specific description whatsoever. He who can meditate on this *nirveda* can transcend the whirlpool of birth and death.

Bhima Bhoi treats *Alekha puruṣa* as his *guru*. He appeals his *guru* in *Stutichintāmaṇi*. 45 to relieve him from the unending suffering that he is facing. He says that he does not want to speak anything more than this.

alekha purusha sriguru mohar mu atai tuma Śisya.
budi maru achhi chhāṇinia mote adhika kahibi kisa.

He further says in *Stutichintāmaṇi*. 58 that *piṇḍa-brahmāṇḍa* belongs to *guru*. It is by his grace on *jiva*, *guru* shall take care of everything.

gurunkara sinā e piṇḍa-brahmāṇḍa āpaṇa āpe bujhiba,
etikimātraka jaṇāuchi muhin jibaku sudayā thiba.

Bhima Bhoi says that if the devotee does not express his suffering before the *guru*, from where he can attain the right knowledge. *Guru* is so compassionate and gracious enough that he can show him the right path.

Guru āge sisya na kahibe jebe kāhun pāiba subuddhi,
sudayāre guru sāgar atanti pratyakṣe karuṇānidhi.

According to Bhima Bhoi *guru-sevā* is the foundation of spiritual *sādhanā*. There is no other *sādhanā* which can have the equal status as *guru-sevā*. In *Stutichintāmaṇi*, 55 boli he glorifies this *sādhanā*,

punya boli jāhāku kahanti guru padasevā mula,
guru sevā binu āau punyamāna nuhanti se samatulya.

Performance of *guru sevā* has divine effect of *Vishnu-rupa* in his body where his body in transformed with prestine glory and at the end he reaches the divine abode. In *Stutichintāmaṇi*, 57 boli Bhima Bhoi explains this state in detail.

Gurusevā kala prāṇinka angare Vishnu-rupa parakāsa,
agnikanti prāya disuthāi kāya ante Vaikuntha bāsa.

In *Bhajanamālā* 1, he says that if you pursue the path of *nirveda* by *ajapa* and meditate upon *arupa* you can attain *sadjñāna* and *mukti* through the *guru*.

adekhā dekhile sāra ajapā japile pāra,
achinhāku chinhi bhaja aṇarupare,
karibāku thile āshā nirveda dharmare pasa
sadjñāna muktipatha guru duāre.

Nāma tattva:

According to Indian spiritual tradition *nāma sādhanā* opens the spiritual door of all aspirants irrespective of caste, knowledge etc. We find *nāmasamkirtana* of Goudiya Vaishnavism as the only method of practising *bhakti*.

Achyutānanda asks in *Jñanapradeep Gitā*, if he is *śūnyapuruṣa* and *alekha* how he can acquire *nāma* and *rūpa*? Balarāma Dāsa answers this question through the Lord himself in *Virāta Gitā*. Lord says that he takes rest in *mahaśūnya* therefore, there is no possibility of having a *nāma* as he is *arūpa brahman.*

mahāśūnyareti biṣrāma,
sethāre kāhin achhi nāma.

Nāma exists prior to *Brahma* and is the source of everything, as found in his *Aṇākāra Samhitā,*

āge helā nāma pachhe helā Brahma
nāmati saburi mula.

The omnipotence and loving nature of *nāma* has been discussed by Jagannāth Dāsa in *Tulā-Bhiṇā*.

nāmare achhi sarva sakti,
nāmare labhe hari bhakti.

Jagannātha Dāsa further says that it is by *nāma-bhakti* or devotion of *nāma* that helps the devotee to attain supreme knowledge.

Harināma bhajithile brahmajñāna pāi,
asesa brahmaṇḍa Pārtha Harināma kahi.

Now, the issue is, if the Lord is *anāma*, *nirākāra* and *nirguṇa,* how can we reach him through *nāma* and *saguṇa?* In spiritual *sādhanā* both are equally important. *Saguṇa* or *nāma* is the first step and after reaching that step we have to ascend to the second step which is *arūpa*. They are like two wings of a bird. It is by both we can have *sadjñāna*. Achyutānanda has made a unique synthesis of both *rūpa* and *arūpa*. He says that *rūpa* shall be revealed from *arūpa* and both are inseparable and similar aspects of the reality.

arupaṛu rupa prakāsa heba,
rupa jāiṇa arupare misiba.
rupa arupa samāna karithibu,
samatā rupare sabu pāibu.

Achyutananda says that meditation on *nāma* is the best possible path for God-realisation. A real devotee is one who opts for *nāma* as his only action.

nāmare beusā kalati jehu,
bhagata madhye tāṇa ate sehu.

The devotee who engages himself on *nāma*-meditation merges in *parama puruṣa* and is relieved from the worldly-suffering. So he says in *Śūnya Samhitā*, that without wandering here and there, concentrate on *nāma*.

nāmaku chinhile bhakta parame misai,
sola bhelāprāya bhabasindhu pāar hoi.
nāma gale rupa kehi na chinhibe āu,
nāmaku na chinhi eṇeteṇe kimpā dhāun.

Achyutananda says that there is no difference between *nāma*(word) and *nāmi* (the object of devotion). The existence of *piṇḍa* is due to *nāma*. There is no relevance of *rupa* without *nāma*. *Rupa* is manifestation of *nāma*. First there was *nāma* and then there was *rupa*. We cannot know *rupa* without recognising *nāma*. He says in *Jñānapradeep Gitā*,

āaghoon je nāma thilā rupaku gadhilā,
rupara bhitare nāma puri prakāsilā.

nāmaku chinhile sinā rupaku jāṇiba,
rupa na heleṇa nāma kāhin bakhāṇiba.

It is through complete devotion of *nāma* that liberation is possible,

nāmaku bhajile sinā gatimukti pāi,
piṇḍaku kāraṇa nāma binu anya kāhin.

Actually *parambrahma* has neither *rupa* nor *nāma* as both transcend time and space. So he is *Arupa* and *Anāma*. He takes the name and form because of his utter grace for the welfare of the devotees. He says in *Chhayālisi Patala*,

prakrut mora nāma nāhin arupa brahma mu bolāi,
arupa rupabanta hoi nāma svarūpe kheluthāi.

Bhima Bhoi though talks of *Śunya Puruṣ* and *Anāma*, he also gives importance to the *nāma* of *mahimā* for the devotees who can comprehend the nature of reality. Bhima Bhoi in *Bhajanamālā*, 38 prescribes *nāma-sādhanā* as the best religious path for the aspirant who is compassionate for all living beings. He says,

nāmare saraṇa jāa jiba pare dayā baha,
e dharmaru sāra āu nāhin na samsāre.

Again he says in *Bhajanamālā*, 33 that *nāma* is so powerful that by *bhajana* of *nāma*, the stone can be transformed to water, dry wood is bloomed and the fools become wise by getting true knowledge about *alekha*.

nāmaku bhajile chinhi pāsāṇa huanti pāṇi
kāstha pallabita go,...
murkha huanti panditā, paānti jñāna hetu chetā...

Bhima Bhoi warns again and again in *B.N. Gita*, XII that mere mechanical repetition of *nāma* without complete devotion and complete surrender you shall not receive grace of the Lord and devotee leads a life of fake devotee resulting in sins. Mere repetition of *nāma* shall not remove your sins as mere repetition of word 'rice' shall not satisfy your hunger.

*rāma rāma boile ki k**shy**aya heba pāpa,*
bhāta bhāta boile ki palāiba bhoka.
ahāra bhakhyile sinā ātmā bodha heba,
nāmaku bhajile sinā mukati labhiba.

While highlighting the glory of *nāma*, Bhima Bhoi says in *Bhajanamālā*, 32 that *nāma* is inseparable from Brahman which is hidden so that we cannot see him with normal eye. He is nearest to us in such a manner that we can see him through our intuitive eye.

brahmapāse nāma achhi ghodāi kari rakhichi,
charmanayanaku na dise kāhāku.
jñāna nayane disai dure nāhin pāse thāi,
chinhi pārile kahanti sudaye go.

Mahimā nāma is the only *nāma* that is saviour and unique in four *Yugas* which gives us *mukti* and make us immortal. The following is mentioned *Brahma Nirupana Gitā*, VII,

*su**ṇ**iluki nirākāra mahimānka reeti,*
mahimā nāmati jehu jibara mukati.
mahimā nāmati jehu charijuge sāra,
mahimā prakāsh hele huanti amar.

So for Bhima Bhoi *nāma japa* (meditating on *nāma*) is the best kind of *dharma* which can be performed by all for attainment of *jivanmukti*.

The devotee who depends on *nāma* becomes a man of equanimity and is not affected by pleasure and pain and he enjoys the greatest pleasure by meditating on *nāma*.

dukha sukhaku samāna maṇuthāi kebe nuhae bimukha,
nāme āsrākari dina banchuthāi bole e mo bada sukha.

Bhima Bhoi repeatedly says in *Stutichintāmaṇi*. 90 to meditate on *nāma* by engaging in his professional work but also keeping in mind the gracious *nāma*.

puṇi kahuachhu he puruṣamāne mahimā nāmaku japa,
bādi brutti karma karuthāa pachhe hrudapadme nāma rakha.

He says in *Bramhanirupaṇa Gitā* I that *nāma* of *mahimā* is a valuable jewel and continuous meditation on *nāma* shall help you to overcome all sorrows and sufferings.

svāmināma alankāra sarvekara nirantara,
tebe se janmakastaru hoeibe pāar.

Though *mahimā* is indescribable and understanding its nature is very difficult as the nature of *mahimā* is vast and deep. *Nāma dharma* is the only means to understand Him as *purnabrahma*.

According to Kabir *nāma* is the life-force of a devotee who can reach his goal by depending on this. *Nāma* is the supreme giver and his glory is boundless. It is through *nāma smaraṇa* and *nāma japa* that the aspirant becomes free from all evil qualities in him. So for Kabir, meditation of *nāma* is the best means in the path of *sādhanā.*

Kabir firmly says "oh! man give up ignorance, surrender and worship the *nāma* uninterruptedly for liberation."

kahat kabir sunahu re prāṇi,
chhādahu manaka bharama
kebala nāma japahure
prāni parahu ek hi saraṇa.

According to Kabir *nāma* is so precious that when a man who meditates on *nāma* with intense love, there is transformation in his personality. It so happens miraculously that pearls (kind words) flow from his lips and his heart glows with diamond which is nothing but ever-glowing Lord.

Kabir Hari ke nāam soon, priti rahe ektār
tan mukhse moti jhare, heera ant na pāar.

Kabir says that our mind is full of gems. If a man uses his mind properly he can discover whole mine of gems. The clue is very simple and that consists in lovingly reciting the *nāma* of the Lord.

Kabeera man parbat hata, ab main pāyā kāni,
tānki lagu sabad kee, nikasi kanchan khāni.

Kabir says that human life is very short and death may come at anytime without information. So one has not to waste his time in laziness or sleep but remain awake and meditate on *nāma* of the Lord at each and every moment.

Kabir nirbhaya Rāma bhaja,
jab lagi deewai bāti

tel ghatyā hāti bujhee
tab sobai din rāti.

Kabir says that there is a stringless musical instrument in our body which sings the name of the Lord ceaselessly and the entire body is pervaded by that which dispels our doubts and makes our roaming mind steady. If one concentrates on that which will lead from imperfection to perfection and thereby there is a transformation of his personality.

Kabir sabad sarir men, bin gun bāje tānti
bāhār bheetar rami rahyā, tāte chooti bhrānti.

According to Kabir all are equal who meditate on the Lord and chant his name. The matter that is present in the container is important rather than the shape, size and quality of the container.

sabei hamre ek hai, jo sumire hari nāma
bastu lahi pahchan ke, bāsan se kyā kāam.

Kabir says that reciting the name of the Lord is the best path than any other path for attaining mercy and protection of the Lord. Therefore take Lord's name with every breath.

sāans sāans sumiran karau, aur jatan kachhu nāhin.

When one truly becomes a devotee and *jñāni* and performs his *niṣkāma karma*, he is liberated from all sorrows and sufferings and becomes a *jivanmukta* or *brahmasvarūpa*.

In the philosophy of Bhima Bhoi one discovers a unique synthesis of knowledge, action and devotion, even though he takes devotion to be the culmination of knowledge and action. Indeed the traditional classification of the yogic paths as *jñāna yoga, karma yoga* and *bhakti yoga* do not hold good here. These are not three exclusive paths leading to perfection but are mutually complementaries, as one sustains the other. This can be seen in the following *bhajan* where he has expressed in *Bhajanamālā* 78.3 about the quintessence of *mahimā sādhanā.*

kale niṣkāma chitta gamiba sehi patha,
hele bhṛtryara bhṛtya labhiba jñāna tattva.

Bhima Bhoi in *Stutichintāmaṇi*. 93 says that one who utters *nāma* and treats others as his own shall be remembered for his nobility as a *sādhu* in all ages. But mere uterance of *nāma* by a person without moral virtues like truth, non-violence, honesty etc. cannot tread the path of spiritual progress and he has to suffer a lot in his life.

mahimā bhajile paraku maṇiba āpaṇāra ātmā prāye,
sādhu hoi marigale kisa helā juga juga kirti rahe.

x x x

satya na prakāsai mahimā bhajile padai adbhuta māda...

x x x

mahimā bhajile chori na chalai na jibe tahinra pāsa...

Therefore, in *Stutichintāmaṇi*, 100 he appeals to all the persons born in this world to meditate uninterruptedly the *nāma* of *mahimā sāgara.*

āhe naraloka je achha samsāre deha dhari achha e martye,
alekha mahimā sāgara nāmaku bhajana kara samaste.

In *Bhajanamālā*, 40 he points out that one who takes resort to the *nāma* attain *mukti* and shall be placed in the abode in *anantagarbha.*

nāma brahme je āsrita pāiba gati mukati,
bhava sāgaru tariba rahiba anantagarbhe.

Similar idea is also found in his book *Nirveda Sādhanā*, 10

nāmati chariyuga satya, nāma nāhin keun krutya
nāma brahmare āsra kara, samsāru jebe hebu pāra.

In *Brahmanirupaṇa Gitā* he says,

Nāmaku dharithile rati, samsaya pakāibu kāti
nāmati amulya ratan, sari nuhai tribhuban.

In *Stutichintāmaṇi* 100 boli Bhima Bhoi appeals all persons to meditate upon the *nāma* of *Mahimā Sāgar*

ahe maraloka je achha samsāre deha dhari achha e martye
alekha mahimā sāgara nāmaku bhajana kara samaste.

In *Bhajanamālā* 40, Bhima Bhoi says that one who takes shelter in *nāma*, he gets liberation and finds place in *Vaikuntha*.

nāmabrahme je pāiba gati mukati,

In *Brahmanirupaṇa Gitā*, 6th Chapter he says,

mahimā nāmati jehu muruchhā na jāe,
dine bhajile brahma baikuntha se pāe.

Those who take resort to *nāma-brahma* and knows nothing else they become fearless and prostitutes and evil-minded persons involved in *nāma-smaraṇa* they get immediate relief from the imminent danger. Bhima Bhoi assures this in *Stutichintāmaṇi* 92 boli,

chhatiskulaje pātaka je achha stiri purusa,
uchha neecha boli grahaṇa na kari nāmare saraṇa pasa.

kiba besyānāri kibā durāchāri kibā pāshāṇḍa puruṣa,
adbhut bipade ghoti āsuachhi beni netre sabu dekha.

In *Bramhanirupaṇa Gitā*, VII he further says,

mahimā nāmati jehu mukati pasarā,
bhaktagaṇamāne karuchhanti āsarā.

In *Stutichintāmaṇi*, 69 he says that *mahimā nāma* can be meditated by one irrespective caste, creed and sex without any prohibition. It simply depends upon the devotion of the aspirant.

jehu ichhā sehu nāmaku bhajile ethi kichhi dosa nāhin,
ke abā stiri ke abā puruṣa je jana pāriba dhyāyi.

Again in *Stutichintamaṇi*, 91 he clarifies that *nāma* of *mahimā* is very vital because there is no other way for liberation except meditation of *nāma* who moves in the world in four *yugas*. Therefore he advises all the aspirants to follow this path.

suṇa sujñajana nāmara mahimā nāma binā nāhin gati,
nāmare ātajāta heuchhanti ehi pruthvi.

He warns in *Brahmanirupaṇa Gitā* that the person who has no *sraddhā* for *nāma*, know that he is just like a demon not a human being.

nāmare jāhār sraddhā nāhin,
asura boli jāṇa sehi.

In *Ādianta Gitā*, he asks the aspirants to give up their egoism and remember again and again *brahma-nāma* and behave like human beings not as animals.

badimā kathā chhāda sabu, brahma-nāmaku kara hetu.
mana bhitare kara bhakti, nāma rahiba jati satee,
manusya janama labhichha, pasu parāye heuchha.

In *Stutichintāmaṇi*. 90 he terms *nāma-sādhanā* as *saraṇa-darsana* which can be practised by surrendering all things attached to the aspirants.

piṇḍa prāṇa dia jāṇa,
nāmare pasa saraṇa.

The Lord loves his devotees just as he is loved by them. Similar views are also expressed in the Gitā and Bhāgavata. In the Gitā, the Lord says,

> My devotees are my heart and soul and I am the heart and soul of my devotees, my mind is wholly occupied by them and their mind is wholly occupied by me.

In the highest state of *bhakti*, the Lord is no more the controller and ruler of the universe but he stands for loving care and protection of his devotees. This is clearly expressed by the Lord in *Srimad Bhāgavata*, 9.4.63

aham bhakta parādhīna hyasvatantra iva dvija
sādhubhirgrastahṛ dayo bhaktirbhaktajana priyaḥ.

(I have no freedom. My heart is in the grip of devotees. I depend wholly upon them; for they love me and I love them.)

This is referred as *parābhakti* in devotional literature. According to *Mahimā darsana* interestingly when one is in the highest state, one sees oneself in everything and everything in oneself. In otherwords one becomes a true *jñāni*. Therefore, every action of such an enlightened one becomes an instance of *niṣkāma karma*. Therefore the state of *niṣkāmabhakti* is nothing other than the *niṣkāma jñāna* and his life becomes a life of *niṣkāma karma*.

Bhakti is a constant activity in a spirit of extreme goodness. *Sādhaka* on one side constantly goes on practising activity in a spirit of detatchment and on the otherside goes on with the development of his personality. A stage comes when a man has cultivated that spirit of activity, he comes to a stage of the total elimination of the ego, when his experience is that of his activities, their fruits and his entire self, is everything for only God, so we can see at the highest stage, *bhakti* and *niṣkāma karma* are one and the same.

•

Bengali Sacred Hymns*

Chittaranjan Bhoi

Bhajan - 1

On the day when there was no earth or land, O brother,
There was none other than the Eternal Being (*Anādi Purusha*).(1)

The Supreme Being rested in the Great Void,
In wonder, the earth emerged-once it had been nothingness.(2)

As the embodiment of Sound, He manifested there,
As the form of Divine Light, He remained in the Void.(3)

From there were born the *Nāda* and the *Bindu*,
And from the body emerged the eternal *Brahma*.(4)

He manifested fully in every heart,
All came to know Him as the Supreme Being.(5)

The Blissful *Brahma*, in oneness confined,
Took on a body — the soul thus defined. (6)

The wise seek not the sky in vain,
For in the womb of infinity lies the Great Void. (7)

In that realm lies the unseen Lord's own abode,
Says Bhima — guarded well from the ignorant and the low.(8)

* Translation of *'Bangala Atha Bhajan'* by Bhima Bhoi

Bhajan - 2

There is no difference between water and wind,
Two boats sail side by side on the same current.(1)

That One is beyond clan and lineage, without any name;
Formless, yet with form — who can truly describe it. (2)

He ears conscientiously the devotee's prayer to obligate
The embodiment of kindness and righteousness descends to liberate. (3)

He who has known the essence of *Brahma*'s eternal life,
Who can truly grasp him—his virtues, his mind, his silence?(4)

The indescribable glory has manifested as a name —
Who can comprehend it or express it in measure ? (5)

The One called *Alekha* (the Ineffable) cannot be captured in writing
Never can He be seen with these physical eyes opening. (6)

Chants, penance, *mantras*, and charms—none of these suffice.
A lightning flash of truth strikes through the eye of wisdom. (7)

Like the full moon, his light now brightly flows—
With unwavering resolve, Bhima walks as Lord's protected servant (8)

Bhajan - 3

Formless, vast, and without a base—
Who can ever truly trace that face?
How shall one owe, what offering can be made,
To one who has no form nor feet. (1)

To touch the skin, the hair, the flesh in delight—
Yet senses are numb, and darkness is tight.
The nameless light has begun to shine,
And the universe is filled with its sign. (2)

Desire cannot bind the desireless one —
Like the yoke cannot harness one without a pair.
Born in a manner beyond knowing,
No human body can contain or express it.(3)

The rag has no end, nor the loincloth any thread—
How shall I tie a knot instead?
When there is no lust, no anger—
Why should illusion bind any longer?
Sleep itself becomes perfect bliss. (4)

He is not a body-bearing man, but the bodiless one—
You won't find him in any sculpted form.
How can I describe His beauty and virtues—
He is untouched by decay, untouched by dust. (5)

The Nameless—how shall I name them?
Formless—they defy all form and color.
Though born, the body did not unfold with the day—
By its very nature, it remains veiled, adorned in illusion.(6)

So many days have passed, listen, O brother—
Who knew what dwelled so deep within?
Dharma incarnate walks the forest path,
Why then is the innocent child forsaken? (7)

With what wealth, with what virtue shall one speak—
Who, upon vision, simply bows in awe?
In the heart, the mark of the Infinite sings,
On every tongue, His name flows and falls. (8)

This world-play is the sport of the Infinite,
Who weaves the countless tales untold.
He who holds both body and cosmos in being,
Calls out—listen, His voice unfolds.(9)

With teeth clenched and tongue held back,
He falls at the feet of the holy ones.
Says Bhima Bhoi — he meditates on the Divine *Guru*,
And weeps again and again, lost in remembrance.(10)

Bhajan - 4

He has taken the form of man, yet none can truly recognize Him—
Lo, that very Lord is now descended upon the earth. (1)

Deluded by illusion, none shall truly know—
In this *Kali Yuga, Brahma* plays His secret show. (2)

Unborn, yet manifest in this dark age of *Kali,*
None could perceive Him with their mortal eyes. (3)

His own form abides upon this earthly realm,
Why then, in this age, do you not seek the cause? (4)

As *Dharma* incarnate stands the Supreme Divine,
Doubt Him not — He is glory's endless shrine (5)

Dwelling in the Ocean of Milk, He came down to this earth below,
At His holy feet, *Annapurna* Devi humbly served in devotion's glow. (6)

The Absolute *Brahman* reveals Himself as a dual form divine,
For salvation, the devotees behold His sacred sign.(7)

Ever I offer my mind at the beautiful feet of the Divine Pair,
Meditating on the *Guru*'s feet, says Bhima, I find shelter.(8)

Bhajan - 5

Salutations to the Void-Dweller, the formless One,
Whose name resounds as the ocean of glory.(1)

He abides in the Great Emptiness — the Unmanifested Being,
Whose name shines forth in the realm beyond creation. (2)

I grasp not the subtle, the formless, the One beyond divide,
Yet someone dwells in man—whom the devout seek and abide.(3)

The wise bow down before the nameless divine,
Whose truth no words can ever define.(4)

Endless is the glory of the Unwritten Name—
Who can speak it with tongue, with teeth, or proclaim? (5)

In every age He comes, by His own sweet will,
Taking a form to redeem the faithful still.(6)

In the ocean of worldly strife, the soul adrift does lie,
Woven in illusion's snare, the self looks on and sighs(7)

Truth's own boat sails on and never sinks,
The Lord Himself rows it, being the helmsman.(8)

The soul draws near where true wisdom flows – the Guru's sacred feet,
At everyone's feet, Bhima Arakhita humbly bows in love.(9)

Bhajan - 6

Who can fathom the count of the ages, O Mother *Annapurna*!
In the eastern realm of *Jambu-Island*, thy lineage began. (1)

The Supreme *Vaishnava*—an ascetic beyond form, a figure of detachment,
He wandered through ancient lands, bearing the new celestial message. (2)

The Beginningless One descended as Buddha divine,
To grace the day once denied to the devotee's shrine. (3)

With incense and flame, with sandal and camphor bright,
They rose with reverence to wash His feet in sacred light.(4)

For a while, the elder's form faded into the void,
The Infinite Lord in silence His shape enjoyed.(5)

No heart's lotus stirred with mindful grace,
In silent sorrow, I bowed—His feet my resting place.(6)

O sages, O wise men, hold not my faults in sight,
Lowly Bhima chants and meditates, on the *Guru*'s feet.(7)

Bhajan - 7

The Lord of the Great Void bears no form or line,
Who can pierce the mystery—ancient, unscribed, divine? (1)

No color, no sign reveals His boundless decree,
Yet within the seven vessels, O friend, He dwells silently.(2)

Who can house the Imperishable, bearing only His Name?
The seekers search within mind and heart—yet still, they roam the same.(3)

The Infinite *Brahman* flows as an unending stream,
He draws the devotee close—bound by love's sacred seam.(4)

The King, O radiant one, has no form or face;
Like the wind, He dwells in silence—leaving no trace. (5)

Beyond form and virtue, He dwells in the unseen,
His nameless presence guides countless masters serene.(6)

He is the formless secret, beyond birth, ever still—
No *Veda* can describe Him, His path eludes the will.(7)

In the dark abyss of the Great Void, He dwells concealed,
Says Bhima — the unseen, the formless, the unadorned revealed.(8)

Bhajan - 8

Now listen, O noble soul, to the tale ever true—
Without devotion to His glory, life cannot renew.(1)

Unwritten, His greatness—boundless and bright,
That *Brahman* has become this endless world of light.(2)

From the womb of glory, He descends—divine and deep,
Brahma, Vishnu, Shiva — from His essence they leap.(3)

From water, from wind, and from the cosmic flame,
The Unwritten has appeared—earth and sky bear His name.(4)

Three mystic powers, their names unwrit, unknown,
Ten million souls through boundless realms are sown.(5)

The formless Master takes an endless shape,
And speaks the *Vedas* none on earth can ape.(6)

In the beginning, the form of *Vishnu* shone forth,
His essence spread throughout the world's wide course.(7)

Says Bhima, the hidden truth once held secure and dictate,
That Supreme Being now walks the earth as man incarnate.(8)

Karma, Jñāna and Bhakti in Philosophy of Bhima Bhoi and Kabir : A Comparative Study

Laxmimani Majhi

In this article, an humble attempt has been made to explain and analyse the concept of *karma, jńana* and *Bhakti* as found in two important saint-poets; Kabir and Bhima Bhoi belonging to 15th and 19th century respectively. Both the poets belong to Indian Santha tradition and both are saints and poets of outstanding repute. They were social reformers who wanted to save the world from the impending danger and clutches of blind-beliefs, idol-worship, rites and rituals and social evils hampering the peace, harmony and stability of the society. Both of them propagated *Bhakti-mārga* as the way to salvation. The first section is devoted to *Santha Tradition*, the second section depicts the significance of *Bhakti*, the third section is about the views of Kabir and Bhima Bhoi on *Bhakti* and the final section is concluding remarks.

Both the poets Bhima Bhoi and Kabir belong to *Santha Tradition*. Here one may ask a question; who is a *Santha* and what is the difference between *Sādhu* and *Santha*. The *Sādhu* is one who seeks for own self-liberation but *santha* stands for a person who seeks for liberation for whole beings. All *Santhas* are *Sādhus* but all *sādhus* are not *santhas*. Some familiar names in Indian *santha tradition* are Tukāram, Nānak, Dādu, Tulsi Das, Alwars, Narshi Mehta, Jñāneswar, Ramānujchārya and Kabir. The Santha tradition in Odisha refers to Sri Chaitanya, Rāirāmananda, Saralā Dāsa, Balarām Dāsa, Atibadi Jagannātha Dāsa, Achutānanda Dāsa, Jasobanta Dāsa and Shishu Ananta

Dasa. Bhima Bhoi's compositions are called as *Bhajana mālā* whereas Kabir's poems are compiled in *Kabir Dohā*.

What then is *Bhakti*? The term *Bhakti* is derived from the root "*Bhuj*" which means to serve (sevā). whose sevā are we going to do? Can there be any service to the highest reality without any intention or purpose? It is the realisation of the reality, who is found everywhere. One who learns becomes a man of information but not of wisdom. We may call him a book-worm (*sāshtra -pandita*). Bhima and Kabir both reject such knowledge.

Jaga padhpadh sab hoe
Hoe na koi pundit
Dhaiakṣara prem kā
Padhe so hoi pundit

The concept of *Bhakti* is closer to *jñāna* (knowledge) and Action (*karma*). Knowledge for the shake of knowledge binds one with the world but one by following the path of devotion realizes his inner self. Thus, *Bhakti* is spiritual realisation; realization of one's own self. He who knows himself, knows that the world is not different from him. In *Gitā*, it is said that "*Śradhābām Labhate Jñāna*" means *Śraddhā* (one's own unconditional self-surrender) is linked with both *karma and bhakti*. It is Sri Aurobindo, who speaks of synthesis of *karma, Jñāna and bhakti* for a yogi. Thus, *bhakti* makes one closer to the reality (*bhagbat*). Again, what is this closeness? *Ādhyātmya yoga* is *samipyayoga. Samipya* means closer to one self as well as Godhead. One's own self is not different from the spiritual reality what is called in *Upanishads* as *Atman* is same as *Brahman.*

Nature of Reality

In Indian Philosophical literature, Brahman is the highest reality. According to Sankara Vedānta *Brahma Satya Jagat mithyā* this universe is being created by the Brahman who is the ultimate reality, we see the ultimate reality through the internal perception (*Dibya Chaksh*u). It is also named by Spinoza as *Natura Naturata* or *Natura Naturans*, like that Bhima Bhoi and Kabir also say that ultimate reality is one that is *śūnya. śūnya* means not a void, rather, it is *Pūrna* or whole. Bhima Bhoi's concept of reality is called as *Mahimā, Alekha, Nirākār* etc. According to Bhima Bhoi *śū*nya-purusha is the ultimate reality of the universe. He is the Creator of the world. *Alekha Mahimā* is the infinite and indeterminate which is the nature of infinite consciousness. We cannot see it by our sense organs. It cannot be expressed in our language. Bhima Bhoi defines him in his "*Stutichintāmaṇi*".

> *"Arupa sarira rupa nahi jara,*
> *kemante chinhibi muhin."*

Piṇḍa -Brahmāṇḍa

Piṇḍa literally means body and *brahmanda* means the world created by the supreme being. Bhima Bhoi and Kabir also accept *piṇḍa brahmāṇḍa* doctrine that which are manifestations of Śunya Purusa. They advocate about the *piṇḍa* and *brahmaṇḍa* as same:

> *Adhei deheachhi, se je na disuchi*
>
> *e piṇḍa- brahmāṇḍa tāar agyan re rahichhi*
>
> *Basilāthāre asesa brahmaṇḍa disichhi*
>
> *Piṇḍa brahmāṇḍaku krupanetre chaunchhi*

Bhima Bhoi has said that every human being has the potentiality to develop into perfection only when the aspirant realizes the identity of the *Piṇḍa and Brahmāṇḍa*. In this context Kabir says,

Sab ghat merasaiyan,

khāli ghat nahinkoya.

Kabir says that *Piṇḍa* and *Brahmāṇḍa* are identical they are one and merge with one another. One has to realise that the *Brahman* is not to be found outside the body.

Role of Guru

The *Guru* is the one who helps the disciples to ascend to the highest level in the path of *sādhanā*. *Guru* is different from the ordinary teacher as he shows the right path of the self - knowledge. The Guru is a spiritual guide who leads the disciples go out of ignorance. A true Guru is one who protects the *sishya* to teach the path of liberation. *Guru* and *shishya* are similar so that they live together and stay together and therefore no discrimination is found between them. Bhima says:

Guru sishya duhen ektvaatanti

Antara maṇibanāhin

Bhima says that *guru* is the path-finder who looks at welfare of the human beings. Bhima Bhoi writes:

Dipa lagile sarva pāi,
samṣāra guru dipa hoi.

It is because of *Guru*'s blessing, I became a poet. Guru is always eager to shower his grace on devotee. As regards to the significance of Guru, Kabir says ;

Guru Govinda donokhadahai

Kaku lāgipāye

Guru tum balihari, Govinda

Diyobataye.

The role of *Guru* is vital for showing him the true path for God realisation. Again, Kabir says :

Satguru ki kripabina,sat ki bhakti nahoye

Mansa bacha karmna, suni lijou sab koye.

Bhima Bhoi and Kabir both emphasized that three modes of yoga of human beings that are reflected in *karma, jñāna* and *bhakti.* A person in order to be eligible for *sādhanā* must be a man with moral qualities like love, compassion, non-violence etc and must conquer anger and infatuation.

Karma :

Bhima Bhoi accepts the doctrine of *karma* that as you sow so shall you reap. It means the virtuous is rewarded and sinner is punished. The law states that even if one does good actions, it leads to bondage, like Gitā, Bhima Bhoi solves the problem by the concept of *niṣkāma karma.* According to Bhima Bhoi, an action in a detached manner does not bind the individual because he gives up the sense of doership. Karma performed in consonance with dharma leads one to the highest goal. Bhima Bhoi believes in the doctrine of *niṣkāma karma.* Bhima says :

Pāpa karithile pāpaku bhunjibe,
punya thile punya bhoga.

Bhima Bhoi says that *karma* leads to bondage and it is not possible to give up *karma* in order to maintain life. Every person has to do there are own duty. Those do-good action, they are rewarded and those work bad they get punishment. Kabir also says that a balance among *karma, jnana and bhakti* leads to a perfect life in the human being. Kabir says that:

Jo jaisa karahi so taspaihai raja ramaniai,
Jaisi kahai so taisikaretarat bar na lagāi.

Kabir says that you will not be bound by the consequence of action if you give up agenthood or the feeling that I am doing this and consequence is the result of my action.

Jñāna :

Bhima clearly says that *Jñāna* is not possible without the grace of the God who cannot be attained by study of scriptures. *Jñāna* results in steady expansion of mind and heart which leads to love for all as he has the vision that everything is the manifestation of the lord.

Kabir says that ignorance cannot be dispelled by the study of scriptures. The darkness of ignorance will be removed by right knowledge.

Bhakti :

A *Bhakta* needs a *Guru*. For following the path of *Bhakti*, a devotee (*Bhakta*) has to take refuge in a *Guru* - the spiritual mentor. A true disciplined *sishya* has to choose a true *Guru*. Even Bhima Bhoi says that guru (*Mahimā Gosāin*) also came to his door step to select a disciple like him and initiate him in *Mahimā Dharma*. As regards to significance of *Guru*, *Kabir* says;

Sadguru Aisa Keejiye, Lobh Moh Bhram Naahin.
Dariya So Nyaara Rahe, Deese Dariya Maahi

Bhima speaks of complete self-surrender at the feet of the Highest Reality i.e., *MahimāAlekha*. Bhima speaks of *Niṣkāma Bhakti* in *Bhajanamālā,32*

Samarpi piṇḍa prāṇa
Dārā sutta bittadhana
Dhari mate udāsina
Niṣkāmamanare he.

Meaning there by; I surrender my heart and soul, my dearest objects like my wife, son, wealth in *niṣkāma* way.

Mahimā Gosāin on the other hand says;
Dekhi ta niskāma bhakti
Ambhe nachhādu tāra kati.

Meaning there by; I (reality) do not leave the company of my *bhakta* finding his *niṣkāma bhakti*. So, for Bhima, *saraṇa* (unconditional self-surrender) and *darshan* (*Jyoti -darshana*) are the ways to attain liberation or realisation of *Alekha*.

Kabir says;

Prabhutā ko sab koi bhajai
Prabhukobhajena koi,
Kaha Kabir Prabhu ko bhajai
Prabhutā Cheri hoi

Everybody is interested for becoming master or controller but nobody prays to *Prabhu* (the reality) who is the real contrller of the Universe.

To conclude, it can be remarked that both Bhima Bhoi and Kabir expressed their concern for upliftment of the entire mankind through their heart-touching *Bhajans* and *Dohās*. Both try to become as simple as possible so as to reach the common mass. *Bhakti* is a means to *Alekha, Nirākāra Brahman*, Kabir speaks of Heighest Reality in the name of *Rāma*. Both believe in *Avatāravāda*. Their *Guru,* is the Saviour of the universe who descends down to earth to mitigate human sorrows and suffering. There is no need to go to temple, mosque, church, to find God. One has to realise that the reality who descends down to earth to redress human sufferings. Both Kabir and Bhima Bhoi are the pioneers of Santha tradition who dedicate their lives for the upliftment of humanity.

REFERENCES :

1) *Santha Kabi Bhima Bhoi*, Kanhu Charan Mishra (1998) Odisha Sahitya Academy, Bhubaneswar.

2) *Mahimā Dharma, Nilamani Senapati*, Dharma Grantha Store, Cuttack.

3) *Kabi Bhima Bhoi O Mahimā Dharma*, Bhagirathi Nepak, (1974) Bhagirathi Prakashan, Bhubaneswar.

4) *Mahima Dharma Dhārā*, Satrughan Nath, Hemalata Press, Bhubaneswar.

5) *Odishāra Mahimā Dharma*, Chittaranjan Das, G. Mohapatra and Co(1997).

6) *God as Śūnya*- Tandra Pattnaik- D.K Print World, New Delhi (2016).

7) *Mahimā Darsana and Bhima Bhoi*, S.C Panigrahi, DSA Utkal University, Bhubaneswar.

8) *Bhima Bhoi Granthāvali* (2019/2020) Pabitra Mohan Nayak, VOI/II, Friends Publisher, Cuttack.

9) *Santha Kabir: Jivani O Padyāvali* (o), Pt. Nilamani Mishra, Kishore Sahitya Mandira Sutahat (2016) Cuttack.

10) *Selected Works of Kabir* Prajapati Prasad Sah, Sahitya Academy, New Delhi (2019).

11) *Kabir Dohabali* (Ed.) Neelotpal, Prabhat Prakashan, New Delhi.

12) *The Vision of Wisdom : Kabir*, Chandan Sinha, Rupa Publication, (2020).

13) *Philosophical Reflections on Bhima Bhoi and Mahima Dharma,* Harish Ch. Sahoo, Kalinga Institute of Social Science, Bhubaneswar, (2022).

•

Stūti Chintāmaṇi : The Master piece of Bhima Bhoi

Satyananda Swain

Bhima Bhoi's Stūti Chintāmaṇi (Gems of Soulful Prayer) is a unique collection of Odia verse. Though treated as a spiritual composition, it has its laudable literary excellence. It has been accepted as the scripture of Mahimā Dharma and used as a devotees' hand book. The socio-cultural bearing and revolutionary zeal with poetic eloquence grant it a high pedestal in the field of creative literature.

Bhima Bhoi is a well-acclaimed tribal poet of Odia literature. He has written devotional songs; *Bhajana, Jaṇāna, Stūti, Gitā* in delicate Odia language. These songs aim at propagating of Mahimā Dharma.

Stūti Chintāmaṇi is not just a collection of stray poems, it is a complete book with 100 cantos with two thousand couplets. This structural aspect and its spiritual fervour tempts us to recall Dante's 'Divine Comedy'. The poet makes a journey across the human society; observes its state of being, invokes the sprit of Mahimā Swāmi and appeals Him to redress the miseries. He receives messages from the God-head and advises the readers to rise in action. He discovers the world in bond and devises means to snap it. Whenever he discovers despondency he arouses the people, whenever he finds corrupt practice he revolts against it. The poet identifies himself with the suffering lot and gets ready to sacrifice his wellbeing for universal welfare:

Monumental miseries of man,
How can one watch and endure
may my soul be condemned for universal welfare.
(*Stuti Chintāmaṇi*)

It has became his credo. This has also been accepted as the testament of Mahimā Dharma. The poet writes in first person as a votary of Mahimā Swāmi for suffering human beings. He advises all the fellow beings to realize the truth and follow the dictates of conscience. He discovers to his utter dismay that the world is shrouded with ignorance and illusion. Taking the advantage of this darkness, clever, wicked people mislead the people at large. The Kings and the priests have become corrupt. So who would save the common folk! They make the people worship the false gods and lead a beguiled life.

As the follower of Mahimā Swāmi Bhima Bhoi realized that the Lord, God the creator of the world is 'one' and irrefutable. He is Alekh, without shape. Gods and goddesses on the otherhand have shape of clay and stone. So he accepts formless God, Mahimā Alekh for salvation. He makes his view loud and clear.

Gods and goddesses are but soil and stone
Hence, I do worship none,
for salvation I beseech Thee
And pray with concentration. (*Stuti Chintāmaṇi* 1/12)

So Bhima Bhoi explains the canons of Mahimā Dharma throughout the book *Stuti Chintāmaṇi*. He proclaims that as a humble follower of Mahimā Swāmi he propagates His commands *(ājñā)*. Moreover, he has studied the ancient Shāstras, Gita and allied scriptures vis-á-vis the dictates of Mahimā Swāmi and the out come of the venture is *Stuti Chintāmaṇi*.

Apart from being the canonical scripture of Mahimā Dharma, this book embraces other branches of learning. Bhima Bhoi makes a deliberate attempt to present an epic poem. So he propagates the concept of creation. This description is biblical in dimension.

After the deluge, the Earth did not exist
Neither air nor water
only existed nameless void
Not a single shape was there! (*Stuti Chintāmaṇi*)

There was only nothingness. Sound emerged from soundlessness of Nothing and gradually shapes followed suite. In other words this world of forms owes its origins to the formless one- *Śūnya Purusha.* The followers of Mahimā, for that reason, concentrate upon this *Śūnya Brahma.* He can be realized through meditation. A seeker can realize Him, through realization of self. Consequent upon this self, seeking one cannot deem any one form as the Absolute as it is a part of the Absolute. Even elements that form the world like fire, air, water, earth and ether cannot be accepted as a substitute of the absolute singularly. In Indian philosophy the fifth element i.e. 'Ether' or 'sound' is deemed as Brahman (*Nāda Brahma*). These philosophers equate sound-cluster OUM with Brahman. Bhima Bhoi indicates to the abode of soundlessness, *Nishabda Mandira.*"

This state (sound) exudes elixir, and honey. One may relish, enjoy it as one sustains life with air or fire but one has to go beyond these mundane elements. All of these emerge from the nameless state; this is nameless absolute: *Anāma Brahma.* He can be realized both inwardly (inside oneself), outwardly in the outer objects. Bhima Bhoi observes :

He is there in the water, soil
Fire, air inside out
The shapeless one is sound and
Air line selfsame felt.
He is small with small and big with big
equal to animate and inanimate
Linked with aversion and affection
you never discriminate. (*Stuti Chintāmaṇi*, Canto 47)

He is beyond human perception when He cannot be thought about as He has neither colour nor sign. In *Kaliyug* this way of life is essential. There is no alternative. In other words, it is the latest phase of realization. So Bhima emphatically avers.:

In this age this only way
has been devised,
There is no essence in any other
salvation and relief all can be had .
It is a firm and austere, for sure.

(*Stuti Chintāmaṇi,* 45/19)

The formless one is ascertained as the supreme deity. So the way to attain Him is to be free from rites and rituals. All the prevalent ways of worship are denounced by Mahimā Dharma. Only a few rules and regulation were formed and propagated for attainment of salvation.

A follower of Mahimā leads an austere life with the motto– "Simple living and high thinking". He is the humblest individual with concern for universal welfare. He is prompted to pray for preservation of humanity at large as Bhima Bhoi pleads for Him – *"Where shall I live, if this great world is destroyed"?* Hence, I pray all the time for preservation of the world. In Mahimā way of life, the individual salvation rests on universal salvation. So a

Mahimā follower prays for universal welfare along with individual welfare. Bhima's argument runs:

Where shall I be
If this world is destroyed,
Hence, to my Almighty Lord
I always do pray. (*Stuti Chintāmaṇi*)

The entire world is an individual's home, it protects and grants shelter. In return, everyone should try to safeguard it. Bhima claims :

I have presumed the universe
as a single room. (*Stuti Chintāmaṇi*).

But people at large are beguiled. They are misled in the name of dharma. They are misguided and consequent upon their misdeeds they would suffer as :

Disease will torment the body
Anxiety will fill the mind
some will die, some will live
without strength of body and mind.
(*Stuti Chintāmaṇi*, 24/6)

This sort of suffering will be intensified till people are conscious. When the consciousness rises above, there would be universal welfare. Then the world will be free of darkness:

Abuse, ego and pride will vanish
A sense of equality will only be there,
When women enlighten men
The age of Truth shall re-appear.
(*Stuti Chintāmaṇi*, 24/18)

To herald such an age of peace and prosperity people should take shelter in Mahimā Dharma. There are less rules and more practices. Hard work and austerity would make people pious and powerful. They would embrace truth, non-violence as a way of life. Peaceful co-existence would be their motto. Benebholence, purity, fearlessness and compassion would be their principal traits. Having these virtues, the Mahimā followers will live humble lives, putting on Saffron cloth.

The followers of Mahimā Dharma are basically egalitarian. They make relentless efforts to narrow down caste difference. Bhima Bhoi makes it clear that the Lord has created only two castes : the male and the female. There is no third caste. One who believes caste-distinction would never get liberation. Seekers of salvation have to go beyond caste discrimination. Indeed, women are to be respected as mothers. The monks must not cast lustful glance at the face of the women. They may look at the feet of women when they serve *bhikshā* (food). Monks, therefore should avoid the pleasure of female companionship at all costs. He allowed disciples of Mahimā to marry, but the husband and wife must lead a life of purity. They may enjoy sex periodically to beget child only. They would be revered as ascetic *(Jati)* and modest *(Sati)*. Thus Mahimā Dharma believes in sex restriction and women emancipation. Women are not allowed to preach Mahimā Dharam as *Mātā* or nun. They are expected to guide the males in the way of Dharma. As women have greater hold on men, they can build up a better social order with disciplined way of life. But Bhima Bhoi was distressed as he faced protest from the feminine section. The uneducated women pleaded that they know how to eat well and dress well. They were after physical beauty. They craved for frequent physical enjoyment. So Bhima Bhoi prayed Lord Mahimā Swāmi to intervene to grant good sense to these women to embrace Mahimā - way of life, the life of control. They should be chaste. No woman should allow the second man to have relationship with her. It is unethical. "How can you keep two swords in a single scabard?" he asked. If a woman does not follow this rule, she is penalized by the divine. Likewise man must not have relationship with more than one woman. He faces several troubles if he womanises, particularly one who makes love with a widow whose husband dies young or faces unnatural death. The poet has used several couplets how to establish the relationship between man and woman in Mahimā Dharma. He concludes that men are expected to be celebate and women are to be modest.

The preachers of Mahimā Dharma faced formidable opposition from people of all walks of life. The elderly men did not accept the concept of *Śūnya* worship. Mahimā Dharma denounced the worship of the gods and goddesses. It rejects the ways of worship and performance of rites. So as this movement did not get popular applause from elderly people. The preachers approached the younger mass. They were restless and did not like to follow the tenets of the new way of life (Mahimā Dharma). They preferred the funs and frolics to the austre way of life under propagation.

It was natural because Mahimā was a movement from shape to shapeless. Age-old worshippers of icons could not think of any abstract ideology. Facing denials from all section of the society, Bhima Bhoi prayed to Mahimā Swāmi to do the needful. He took the lead in course of time in the company of Govinda Bābā, Nrushigha Bābā. Gradually a good number of saints followed the Mahimā order. Mahimā Dharma made rapid progress under their leadership. They were accepted as the *guru* of the mass. Bhima Bhoi advised the disciples to treat these

Siddha Sadhus with due reverence. These monks were peripatetic. They spent only one night at a place or in a village and accepted only one meal from a householder. They did not establish any lasting relationship with the devotees except spiritual. They took bath long before sun rise and prostrated seven times before the *Śūnya*. They prostrated in the same manner in the evening for five times. Devotees and disciples followed suite reluctantly. But those who took it, they embraced it to their hearts. The doctrines of Mahimā Dharma have been explained in the book, *Stuti Chintāmaṇi*. The poet presents how the people in general were taught the canons of the Dharma.

If you embrace the non-violent cult
Be non-violent all the while,
If you become violent, even for the Guru
By providence you will be penalized.

(*Stuti Chintāmaṇi,* 81/14)

Almost all the dicta of the way have been briefly discussed in this poetical work. But they have not been systematically arranged to be treated as philosophy. There is much of emotional flow which cause spiritual sparks. So the followers of Mahimā Dharma read the *Stutis* with devotion but do not follow it verbatim as religious canons.

Bhima Bhoi has used myths of Hindu scriptures. The Gods and Goddesses have been presented with their power and profile. Today they are worshipped with forms. Though Bhima Bhoi categorically denounces them at a particular point but adores them in another. This creates confusion in the religious or spiritual understanding. Bhima might have incorporated the traditional godheads for spiritual understanding or explanation. However, he has tried to redefine their status. For example, Ramachandra is otherwise known as Dāsarathi. Lexically this means son of Dasaratha, Ramachandra of Ayodhya. But Bhima poetically elaborates :

Darshan matrake prasanna huante
Teṇu nama Dāsarathi. (*Stuti Chintāmaṇi*)

As one is pleased at a glance he is called Dāsarathi. It has no logical point. Some such leapses have been overlooked as poetic overflow of emotion.

In case of writing poetry of epic dimension, the poet lapses into autobiography when he runs short of inspiration or facts of the narrative. In case of Bhima Bhoi, the observation proves true. Bhima narrates his early days in details in the poem. He used to take care of cows and calves in the jungle. He lived half clad and half-fed. He prayed the Lord being hungry and destitute. He could get the vision of Mahimā Swāmi in the village he lived in. By that time, the strange looking mendicant was asking for food and drinks but people did not respond to Him. Bhima repented in the later years personally for such apathetic attitudes of villagers. Mahimā Swāmi called him and granted him poetic powers. He directs Bhima to write on his *Bhajans*. The Lord Mahimā Swāmi left Bhima at home and moved about preaching Mahimā Dharma. He set up *Dhunis* and instructed the monks to preach for the śūnya- worship at different places. Bhima Bhoi wrote and sent his *bhajans* to his Guru Mahimā Swāmi for aproval.

During that time something unwanted happened. Bhima Bhoi was distracted from the path of complete renunciation. He was given with a family as wished by him. He wondered at the ways of the divine because such people are expected to renounce the world. He wrote,

People become monks
Renouncing the native places
where in scripture it is stated
That they accept wives and issues?

(*Stuti Chintāmaṇi*, 4/64)

Bhima Bhoi knew the secret. So he did not become a monk. He became a devotee instead and enjoyed the domestic duties. Bhima Bhoi realized the nature of his happiness.

What unjust deed I did
What irrational thing was done ?
Lord Alekh gave me everything
As I am devoted to Him.

(*Stuti Chintāmaṇi*, 9/64)

Bhima Bhoi knew the austere ways of the Mahimā monks. They are spiritual volunteers for self-extinction without attachment. But devotees can live a life with wife and children. So Bhima deemed himself as a devotee. As a special devotee he accepted adoration and enjoyed life of abundance. He considered it as divine favour and did not care for the critics. He presented himself as the son of the Lord. So, the property he enjoyed was his due. He considered himself as son of the Lord of the world and naturally had authority over everything. He moved to the point of acceptance from the point of abstention. People became jealous of Bhima Bhoi as he was adored by people in general. Women of high caste worshipped him with flower and sandle-paste. He enjoyed fabulous prosperity. Bhima Bhoi was confirmed that he was just. All those were outcome of the divine grace. He did not pay any heed to the criticism of the people who found fault with him . He deemed this public opinion as the voice of jealousy. So he made up his mind to preach to those who worshipped him. He refused his aspiration for monkhood. He declared not to put on the bark of *Kumbhi*. He taught his followers the ways of virtue and religion as much as he practised himself.

He presented Mahimā Dharma as everyones' religion. People of all walks of life can practice it. So he opined that people need not change their profession to embrace Mahimā way of life. He advised the fishermen to chant the glory of Mahimā while catching fish. A soldier may kill enemies in the battle-field, even he can kill cows but he can chant Mahimā and be inworldly non-violent. They do not kill any one out of animosity. It is a way of life that complements a social structure.

A Mahimā-minded man has a value-oriented mind. He admires and practices values like, truth, peace, mercy, kindness, humanism and brotherhood. Whatever a Mahimā follower does has a universal appeal. For him the universal welfare is the uppermost and individual welfare is included in the act of the performer.

Though Mahimā way of life appears common place and lowly, it is magnificent and broad. The performers are down to earth but their thoughts are sky high. While tilling the plot of land a farmer feels that he is working for the world. He serves the Lord of the world. We are the servants of the Lord. We are paid by him, our labour contributes to the store of the world. He does not have narrowness of mind. He does not try to get something at other's expenses. Rather he works in such a manner that the world will be richer at his expenses, Bhima Bhoi was filled with remorse at the sight of encircling distress. He got ready to renounce his wellbeing for the better of the world.

All the devotees are expected to be brothers and sisters. There is natural respect and love for each other. Hence the society of the devotees is well organized. They pay respect to one another and shout '*Saraṇa*' at one's appearance. All the devotees pay respect to the mendicants as the representative of the *guru*. In the evening after prayer they assemble on the premises of the tungi of the mahimā ashram and sing *bhajanas* accompanied by *gini* and *khajani*.

The Gurushisya relationship is incredibly close in this worship of the void. Only men of realisation can experience it. Bhima Bhoi elaborates :

With prestine love they are tied
There is no other bond
He does not desert the devotee.

(*Stuti Chintāmaṇi,* 88/12)

Marking the bond among devotees and that between the Lord and the devotees Bhima Bhoi becomes optimistic and encourages the followers to cling closer for the salvation :

If all will serve the gurudharma
All will be saved,
If virtue grows with piety
Generations of men will be rescued.

(*Stuti Chintāmaṇi,* 67-11)

A good number of faiths had been preached and practised in Odisha. The religious minded Odia people had respect for all of them. It is well marked that people of almost all the religious sects live together in Puri in particular and Odisha in general. The Mahimā order was the latest of all. So Bhima

Bhoi made comparative statements upon them. He made it clear that Mahimā Dharma is not like one of the cults or ways. It is totally different. It is not the worship of snakes or yoginis. It is not worship of Siva either. It is different and acceptable as it is based on rationalism. Moreover it is a way of life that has reduced rituals and discarded blind beliefs. Even then Bhima advised people to embrace it for happier and longer life.

Whatever is called virtue
Is nothing but service to the perceptor
No other way is as good
or equal in any measure. – 16

Other ways can be easily performed sacrifice to the preceptor cannot be easily done.

Being vain, many have died
Assuming themselves great and benign. – 17

(*Stuti Chintāmaṇi,* Canto 55/16/17)

Throughout the poem Bhima Bhoi narrates the inception of Mahimā order in the world for salvation of the world. He makes a physical as well as spiritual journey for realization of Truth for liberation of physical bond, social strains and spiritual crises. His prayer for self- realization is based on selfless consideration. His prayer is intense enough to involve the spirit of the ETERNAL:

1. O Shapeless one, O Lord of the void
   Pay heed to my prayer
   I do relate all to thee
   As you are the great Lord and master.

2. I prostrate at your feet
Keeping hands on head,
Mercifully grant one wish
O'Alekh the dweller of the void.

3. You brahma perfect, righteousness perfect
There is perfect truth everywhere
you are kindness perfect forgiveness perfect
Peace perfect and all…

x x x

5. You are perfect knower of our inner thoughts
As you are omniscient
You are capable of managing well and woe
of the fifty-six-crore occupants.

6. For that reason I pray so much
To the mighty Lord
For all who have embraced
Alekh Mahima Order
And

20. May Gurudharma rise
Truthful religions be enhanced
Bhima Bhoi wishes this much
May not people be tormented by cupid.

(*Stuti Chintāmaṇi,* canto 96)

With this prayer to Almighty Alekh Mahima, Bhima Bhoi completes *Stuti Chintāmaṇi* for universal welfare and naturally acclaims universal adoration without reserve.

References :

1. Swain, Satyananda (Ed.) *Jagata Uddhār Heu, Bhima Bhoinka Strestha Kāvyakrūti*, New Delhi – National Book Trust, India, 2014. (Odia).
2. Swain, Satyananda (Translation) *Bhima Bhoi's Stuti Chintāmaṇi* (English) Bhubaneswar, Odisha Sahitya Akademi, 2020.

•

CONTRIBUTORS

Pabitra Mohan Nayak was born in Subarnapur (Sonepur) district. He obtained Ph.D. From Sambalpur University in English literature. As an educational administrator, he worked as the Registrar in Berhampur and Sambalpur University. While he was the Principal of Sonepur College, he was fascinated towards the writings of Bhima Bhoi, most popular poet of the soil. His books like *Subaltern Voice* (2016), *The Voice of Silence; Sonepur Durbar and Indian Cultural Traditions* (2001) depict a clear viewpoint of Bhima Bhoi's struggle for the upliftment of the downtrodden class and establishment of an egalitarian social order. M/s. Friends publisher, Cuttack has published two volumes of "*Bhima Bhoi Granthābali.*" Vol – I (2018), Vol II – (2020), edited by Prof. Nayak.

Ishita Banerjee – Dube is Professor of History at Centre for Asian and African Studies, E.I. Colegio de Maxico. As a front line researcher in the field of religion with special reference to Mahimā Dharma, her works include '*Divine Affairs : Religion, Pilgrimage* and the *State in Colonial and Post-colonial India* (Simla, 2001) *Religion, Law and Power* (Anthem Press – 2009) and *Ancient to Modern : Religion, Power and Community in India* (Co-edited) Oxford University Press (2009).

Dhaneswar Sahoo : With an outstanding academic carrer servced in Odisha Education Service (Govt. College Branch) for thirty three years. He is a prolific writer, noted columinist, acclaimed social reformer and by choice a rationalist. For his creative essays, he has been awarded by Odisha Sahitya Academy (2010), Perriyar International Award (2014) and Govt. of Odisha Senior Group Literary Award (2017). His works include; *The Concept of Descriptive Metaphysics*, *Sanskruti Jijñāsā* (O), B. R. Ambedkar's *Castes in India* (Odia Translation) and *Abraham Kavoor* (O) etc.

Harischandra Sahoo The Editor of the present volume was former Professor, Bhima Bhoi Research Chair, KISS DU Bhubaneswar. He has served for 37 years as teacher of philosophy in O.E.S. His Ph.D. Work has been published as *"Dream and Sleep : A Study in Philosophy of Mind"*. He depicts the cultural heros of Odisha in the volume *"Iconic Figures of Modern Odisha"* published by Black Eagle, America. His edited books on Bhima Bhoi are (1) *The Philosophy of Bhima Bhoi and Mahimā Dharma (2) Philosophical Reflections on Bima Bhoi and Mahimā Dharma (3) Divyadṛusta Bhima Bhoi (4) the Mahimā Gadi & Tungis in Odisha* . He has edited some text books in Philosophy which are prescribed for the University students like *Contemporary Indian Philosophy, Ethics : Theory and Practice, An Introduction to Practical Ethis etc.*

Subhasis Sahoo is presently Assistant Professor at the Department of Sociology, Central University of Allahabad. Dr. Sahoo is the recipient of prestigious Professor M. N. Srinivas Memorial Award for young sociologist; Professor Radhakamal Mukherjee Memorial Award for Young Social Scientist and International Visiting Faculty Fellowship of Bielefeld University, Germany. His writings have been appeared in three languages including English, Hindi and Odia. He has published more than thirty research papers in reputed national and international journals like *Indian Journal of History of Science*, *International Journal* *of Contemporary Sociology* and edited volumes including Routledge, Springer, Sage, Gyan, TERI and DST, Govt. of India.

Sital Mohanty is currently Assistant Professor at the Department of Sociology, School of Liberal Studies, KIIT University, Bhubaneswar. She was a Post-Doctoral Fellow (2020-23) at NISER, Bhubaneswar and Visiting Scholar at Madras Institute of Development Studies (MIDS), Chennai. She has research publications in reputed national and international journals including *Review of Development and Change*, *Journal of Human Values*, *Social Change*, *Sociological Bulletin*, *The Eastern Anthropologist*, *Social Science Gazetteer* among others and several edited volumes including Routledge and Mittal.

Chittaranjan Misra After a teaching career ranging over more than three decades he was retired as Head, Department of English, B.J.B. Autonomous College, Bhubaneswar. He has authored six anthologies of poems in Odia and two in English. He has translated Camus' novel "*The Outsider*" and four plays of Harold Pinter into Odia. Author of seventeen books including his research based work "Harold Pinter: The Dramatist" Dr. Misra has published his poems and papers in National and International journals. He has lectured on the Nobel British Dramatist Harold Pinter as a guest speaker in the University of Jean Moulin, Lyon, France in 2007. He has edited critical essays entitled *"Indian Writing in English : Odishan Contribution"* in 2015. In 2019 he has edited an anthology titled *"Resonance : English Poetry from Poets of Odisha"* published by Authors Press, New Delhi, His poetry collection "*Lies of Limerence*" has come out in 2020.

Anjali Mohapatra was formerly Head of Department of Philosophy, Ravenshaw (A) College, Cuttack. She has retired from Govt Service (College Branch) as OES (I). Her works include : *Srimad Bhāgavata of Jagannātha Dasa : A Philosophical Perspective* and *The Concept of Action and Agent in Gitā*.

Sarat Chandra Panigrahi retired fom Utkal University as Professor and Head. P.G. Deptt. of Philosophy. He is a well known writer in the academic circle as a prolific writer and a teacher par excellence. He is the author of many books like: *Self-Knowledge, Issues in Indian Ethics, Bhima Bhoi and Mahima Darsana, Concept of Yoga in the Gita. The Philosophy of Bhagavad Gita, Life and works of Gautam Buddha (O), Life and works of Mahabir Jaina (O), Guru Nanak Jibana O Darshna (O) and Drusti Darsanare Kabir Gāhā (O)*. At present, he is Professor Emeritus in KISS Deemed to be University, Bhubaneswar.

Chittaranjan Bhoi is a well-known scholar, teacher, literary critic and translator in English language. He is a man of commitment to academic excellence. At present he is working as Head of Dept. of English, KISS DU, Bhubaneswar. He is the Director HRDC in addition to his academic assignment. He is head of the department of Centre for Translation Studies and as Dean of School of Comparative Tribal language. His works includes *The Rhetoric of Resistance : An Apprisal of John Osborne's Plays, Hundred Years of Odia Poetry* (A Translation of Odia Poems) and *Gopabandhu Das's Poems in Translation* (Bandira Ātmakathā and Kārā Kabitā).

Laxmimani Majhi is a Research Scholar on the Philosophy of Bhima Bhoi and Kabir. She is at present doing her Ph.D. in KISS D.U. Bhubaneswar. She has participated in several seminars and symposia.

Satyananda Swain is a recipient of Kalinga Sahitya Academy and Mukti Translation award. He retired from service as a Reader in English and his areas of interest is Indian English Literature, especially the novels of R.N. Tagore. He is a prolific writer and his works are *Mahima Concept of Salvation, Mahimā Papers, Jagata Uddhāra Heu, Sārā Jibana Jorandā Jātrā, Priya Mahasaya and Riti, Niti, Parichiti* etc. He is the Editor of Odia Journal *Samarpana*. His recent work is the translation of Bhima Bhoi's *Stuti Chintamaṇi*, published by Odisha Sahitya Academy, Bhubaneswar.

•

www.ingramcontent.com/pod-product-compliance
Lightning Source LLC
Chambersburg PA
CBHW010939120626
46554CB00008B/2532
* 9 7 8 1 9 9 8 4 7 5 9 9 5 *